THE GREAT TIN CRASH
BOLIVIA
AND THE WORLD TIN MARKET

Latin America Bureau

First published in Great Britain in April 1987 by
Latin America Bureau (Research and Action) Limited
1 Amwell Street
London EC1R 1UL

British Library Cataloguing in Publication Data

Crabtree, John
   The great tin crash : Bolivia and the world tin market.
   1. Tin miner and mining --- Bolivia
   I. Title II. Duffy, Gavan III. Pearce, Jenny IV. Latin
   America Bureau
   338.2'7453'0984

   ISBN 0-906156-29-7

Written by John Crabtree, Gavan Duffy and Jenny Pearce.
Cover photograph by Julio Etchard, design by Sergio Navarro.
Map by Michael Green © Latin America Bureau
Trade distribution by Third World Publications, 151 Stratford Road,
Birmingham B11 1RD
Distribution in USA by Monthly Review Foundation
Typeset, printed and bound by Russell Press, Nottingham

Contents

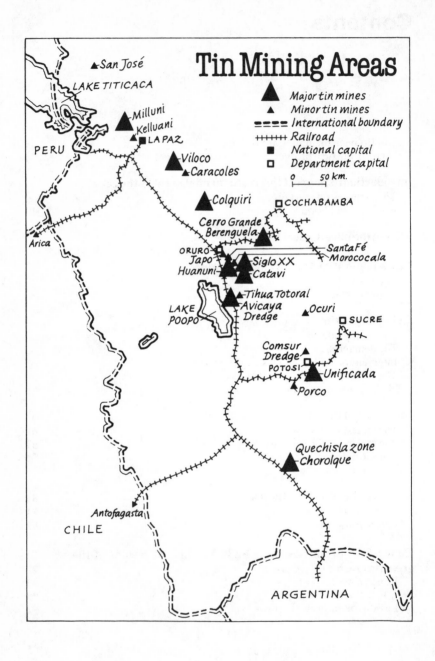

Tin Mining Areas

▲ Major tin mines
▴ Minor tin mines
===== International boundary
++++++ Railroad
■ National capital
□ Department capital

0   50 km.

San José

LAKE TITICACA

Milluni
Kelluani
LA PAZ

PERU

Viloco
Caracoles

Colquiri

COCHABAMBA

Cerro Grande
Berenguela

Arica

Santa Fé
Morococala

ORURO
Japo
Huanuni

Siglo XX
Catavi

Tihua Totoral
Avicaya
Dredge

Ocuri

SUCRE

LAKE
POOPO

Comsur
Dredge
POTOSI

Unificada

Porco

Quechisla Zone
Chorolque

Antofagasta

CHILE

ARGENTINA

Bolivia profile

Area:	1,098,581 sq km
Population:	Total 6.3m (1984)
	Urban 29% (1960); 47% (1984)

Principal towns: (population 1984)

La Paz	881,404	— seat of government
Santa Cruz	376,912	
Cochabamba	281,962	
Sucre	79,941	— legal capital

The people

Origins: Amerindian 55%, Mestizo 20-30%, White 5-15%
Language: Quechua, Aymara, Spanish
Life expectancy: 54 (1984)
Infant mortality: 124.4 per 1,000 live births (1982)
Population per doctor: 1,952 (1980)
Literacy: 62.7% (1980)

Labour force (1980)

Agriculture	56.1%	Construction	4.7%
Manufacturing	10.5%	Mining	2.8%
Others	25.9%		

Economy

	1982	1983	1984	1985	1986
			(growth rates)		
GDP at constant 1980 prices	−4.8	−7.3	−3.2	−4.1	−2.9
Agricultural sector	−2.2	−22.0	3.5	−	−
Manufacturing sector	−15.3	−7.5	−6.6	−	−
Construction sector	−40.0	0.0	−20.2	−	−
Mining	−9.4	−0.4	−15.5	−	−

GDP per capita: US$540 (1984)

Inflation

1979	45.5%	1982	296.5%	1985	8,163.4%
1980	23.9%	1983	328.5%	1986	66.0%
1981	25.2%	1984	2,177.2%		

Real wages (growth rate)

1979	1.4%	1982	−27.1%
1981	−8.7%	1983	−2.5%

Trade exports		*Imports*
US$909m	1981	US$680m
828m	1982	429m
755m	1983	473m
724m	1984	412m
580m	1985	430m

Major exports

Natural gas 46%; tin 25.2%; other minerals (wolfram, antimony, lead zinc, copper, silver, bismuth, iron, gold, etc) 13.6%; sugar 3.2% (1983); cocaine (worth approximately US$2 billion in 1985).

Major trading partners

Exports to: US 33%; Argentina 15%; UK 9%, Brazil 5% (1980)
Imports from: 28%; Japan 18%; Argentina 11%; Brazil 9%; West Germany 8% (1980).

Tin production (in tonnes)

1981	29,781	1984	17,000
1982	24,660	1985	16,136
1983	26,660	1986 (est)	10 − 12,000

Tin producers in Bolivia

Comibol 70% medium-sized companies 20-25%; small firms (production up to 100 tonnes) 5%.

Foreign debt (public)

1979	US$1,941m	1983	US$2,780m
1981	US$2,450m	1984	US$2,797m
1982	US$2,373m	1985	US$3,190m

Debt per capita: US$541 (1985)

Debt service as ratio of total exports

1979	18.1%	1983	44.4%
1981	32.1%	1984	63.1%
1982	43.5%	1985	60.0%

Sources: World Development Report, World Bank, 1986; *Economic & Social Progress Report in Latin America,* Inter-American Development Bank, 1985; *World Development Report,* World Bank, 1983; CEPAL Economic Survey, Comercio Exterior, Banco Nacional de Comercio Exterior, Mexico 1984; *South; Third World Magazine;* CEPAL Economic Survey volumes 1 and 2; tin production figures from Medium Mining Companies Association, Bolivia; IMF Survey

Introduction
The great tin crash: tin miners carry the can

In October 1985 the price of tin fell by half, from just over £8,000 to less than £4,000 per tonne (see chart on page 5). The International Tin Council (ITC) — the 22-nation body made up of both consumers and producers which administered the International Tin Agreement (ITA) and whose job was to keep the tin price stable — had run out of money, owing about £900 million to bankers and metal traders. The international tin market collapsed. In March 1986, after all efforts to rescue tin trading had failed, the London Metal Exchange (LME) terminated its tin contract.

The tin market had been oversupplied and therefore out of balance for some years, but the crash finally came about for an unusual, even technical reason: sudden changes in dollar and sterling exchange rates (see chapter 2). Because of the collapse of the tin agreement, the ITC stocks of tin, equal to about six months of consumption, became available to the market and are likely to depress prices for some time to come. As a result, 'adjustments' in the tin market which would have taken years are now happening very rapidly. The hardship for the mining communities which are bearing the burden of these 'adjustments' — ie mine closures — is very great.

Around the world, from the Siglo XX mine in Bolivia to Geevor in Cornwall, thousands of tin miners are losing their jobs. Many are from poor countries or regions where few alternative forms of employment exist. Bolivia is now second only to Haiti as the poorest country in the Western hemisphere. Many tin miners are leaving their company-owned homes for an uncertain future in the cocaine-producing areas. Although threatened by anti-drug campaigns, thousands of Bolivians already have no alternative means of making a living; their numbers are growing as the tin industry collapses. Those who remain in the mining towns are living on one meal a day of bread with bean and potato peelings. Children are falling asleep at their desks from malnutrition and miners have been going to work on near empty stomachs in a bid to prove that the mines are worth saving.

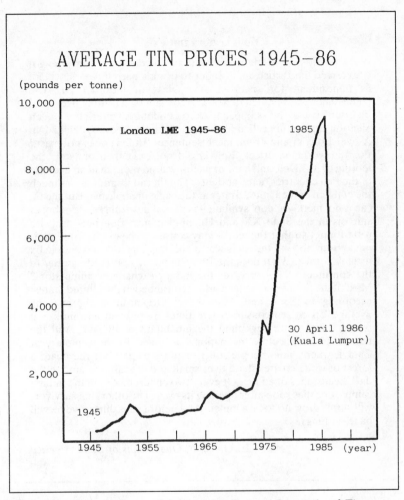

AVERAGE TIN PRICES 1945–86

(pounds per tonne)

London LME 1945–86   1985

1985

30 April 1986
(Kuala Lumpur)

1945

1945   1955   1965   1975   1985   (year)

October 1985: the collapse of the tin price. Source: *International Tin Council.*

The per capita GNPs of the world's major tin producers range from US$540 for Bolivia and Indonesia, to US$860 and US$1,980 for Thailand and Malaysia respectively. In contrast, the major consumers of tin are all developed countries; the USA alone uses more than the total third world consumption of tin metal. The average per capita income in the USA is US$15,390. People living there are thirty times better off than the Bolivian miners who are bearing the cost of the tin crash.

Bolivia does not exist

A story is told of Mariano Melgarejo, a dictator of a century ago, who forced the British ambassador to drink a barrelful of chocolate as punishment for sneering at a glass of local *chicha*. The ambassador was paraded down La Paz' main street sitting backward on a donkey and then shipped back to London. An infuriated Queen Victoria supposedly called for a map of South America, chalked an *X* over Bolivia, and pronounced sentence: 'Bolivia does not exist.' For the world, in effect, Bolivia did not exist then or later: the looting of its silver, and later of its tin, was no more than an exercise of the rich countries' natural rights. The tin can is, after all, as much the emblem of the United States as the eagle or apple pie. But the tin can is not merely a 'pop' symbol; it is also, if unwittingly, a symbol of silicosis in the Siglo XX and Huanuni mines: Bolivians die with rotted lungs so that the world may consume cheap tin. Tinplate is made from tin, and the tin is worth nothing: a half-dozen people fix its global price. What does the Bolivian miner's bitter life matter to the consumer of preserves or the money-exchange manipulators? Most of the tin refined in the world is consumed in the United States: according to Food and Agriculturel Organization figures, the average US citizen consumes five times more meat and milk and twenty times more eggs than the inhabitant of Bolivia. And the miners are well below the national average. In the cemetery at Catavi, where blind people solicit pennies to pray for the dead, a forest of white crosses stand over small graves scattered among the dark headstones of adults. Of every two children born in the mining camps, one dies soon after opening its eyes. The other, the survivor, will surely grow up to be a miner. And before he is thirty-five he will have no lungs.

E. Galeano, *Open Veins of Latin America*

The tin price declined to £3,400 per tonne in the middle of May 1986 climbing slowly back to £4,500 by the end of 1986. This is far below average break-even costs for the industry. High-cost producers will not survive at these prices. It is estimated that the break-even point of mines which must stay in production to satisfy consumption is about £6,250 to £6,750 per tonne. At greatest risk is Bolivia. Even before the tin crash, the state mining company was making heavy losses. The President of Bolivia, Victor Paz Estenssoro, has claimed that mining tin costs the country ten times more than it would cost to leave it in the ground. He has declared the tin era over in Bolivia and announced plans which, it was first stated, would halve the workforce. By the end of 1986 it was clear that job losses would be far greater than this: 18,500 miners and other employees of the state mining company, Comibol, have lost their jobs, out of a workforce which had stood at 27,600 in August 1985 (ie 70 per cent of those previously employed by Comibol). These figures speak of a national tragedy.

In line with their legendary tradition, Bolivia's miners have once again mobilised against government policies. At the end of July 1986, they began a series of labour stoppages, hunger strikes and marches. In August 20,000 miners went on strike. A few weeks later, 100 families occupied the Siglo XX mine in the southern province of Potosi and 5,000 miners and their families from Oruro and Potosi organised a 'March for Life and Peace'. The 150-mile protest march, from Oruro to La Paz, was stopped by the army fifty miles from the capital. The government declared a ninety-day state of siege and arrested about 160 opposition leaders. The leadership of the Bolivian Workers Congress, the COB, went into hiding. In September, many miners went on hunger strike when miners' leaders signed an agreement with the government, an agreement which was subsequently rejected by the rank-and-file. The miners are much weakened by their fall in numbers and the virtual collapse of the country's state mining industry. A hunger strike in December called on the government to fulfil its promises of compensation to those laid off. But the miners' union remains committed to the defence of a nationalised mining industry.

The miners argue strongly that Bolivia's tin industry can be saved, that Bolivia's economy, already in ruins but for the illegal earnings of the cocaine trade, must preserve its productive base. The miners took on this task, given the attitude of the government, in a bid not just to protect their own livelihoods but also to secure a future for Bolivia. The miners' fight is, however, very different from their many previous battles. The traditional weapon, withdrawal of labour, is not effective when the government wishes to close mines. This time, the miners are not only confronting their usual enemy, the Bolivian army, they are taking on an ultimately more powerful and intractable force: the world market.

The ability of the Bolivian government to implement the seemingly compelling logic of the world market is greatly stengthened by the way in which that logic pits worker against worker around the globe. From Thailand to Cornwall, workers have demanded subsidies to keep production going until the excess stocks still dominating the market are run down, and the tin price rises. But maintaining the tin supply itself delays the rise in prices; it may not ultimately prevent mines from being forced out of business.

In Thailand, the impact of the crash was first felt by small companies which specialised in smuggling to avoid ITC production quotas. They were soon put out of business by the collapse of the tin price. Bigger mines were also soon hit, especially those operating large dredgers to scoop up deposits on the country's southwest coast. By September 1986, 40 per cent of Thailand's 630 active mines were estimated to be out of action, although very few closures were reported officially. Many of those still in production had cut their working day from sixteen hours to ten. One estimate suggests that at least half of the country's 32,000 miners are likely to lose their jobs as a result of the crisis.

By January 1986, only 280 of Malaysia's 450 mines were still operating. The workforce in the industry had fallen from 23,000 to 16,000. By September 1986, only 187 mines were left in operation, employing just under 12,000 workers. Both the Thai and Malaysian governments announced short-term relief measures in the belief that the price of tin would soon rise again. The Malaysian government introduced a soft loan scheme, compensating miners when prices fell below a specified floor. This is expected to prevent around 110 mines from closing and will save some 5,000 jobs.

Only Indonesia, one of the lowest-cost producers, embarked on an aggressive strategy of expanding output and lowering costs to maintain employment. But the country's economy is already in great difficulties with the fall in oil and gas prices and it could not afford to subsidise the industry indefinitely.

In Britain, Cornwall is another victim of the tin crash. Registered unemployment in the region was 20.5 per cent (30,000 people) in 1986, and the collapse of the tin price has been a major blow to job prospects there. Cornwall's mines are also high cost, and although in recent years production has recovered from previous difficulties, this was largely due to the high price of the metal on world markets. Tin is Cornwall's second largest industrial employer, providing 1,500 jobs directly, with many traders and service industries also depending on the tin industry. Cornwall County Council estimated that if the mines were to close, unemployment would rise to 27 per cent in the county as a whole and from 26 to over 47 per cent in the area around St Just, where Geevor — Cornwall's only remaining independent tin company — is situated. In August 1986, the Thatcher government agreed, mostly for political reasons, to subsidise two of the region's mines. 'This is a remarkable moment', said the late Liberal MP for Truro, David Penhaligon. 'It is the first time this government has given a farthing to anything but a bank since 1979.'

Both mines were owned by Rio Tinto Zinc (RTZ), a large and powerful multinational company. RTZ could easily have subsidised the mines itself; in 1985 it announced increased profits of £236 million. Only 640 jobs have been saved by the government's subsidy, and a few more at supplier companies. Geevor had requested £20 million over four years as the cost of its survival. While this was refused, the British government offered £50 million towards its share of the ITC's debts. Government concern for the damage to the LME and the City of London as a result of the ITC's default was evidently far greater than for the livelihood of hundreds of tin miners. The management of Geevor subsequently offered the mine for use as a dump for radioactive nuclear waste.

The Great Tin Crash examines the tin crisis from the point of view of those who will lose most from the changing fortunes of tin — the tin workers and their families. It is they who will ultimately pay the greatest price for the adjustments now taking place in the tin market as high cost producers are forced out of production. Chapter 1 looks at the present situation in the Bolivian mining areas; how communities, long accustomed to poverty and deprivation, now face the most serious threat yet to their meagre livelihoods.

Tin on the world markets

The tin workers are caught up in the volatile and complex world of mineral commodity markets, which operate according to a logic which has no time for the personal tragedies and hardship it may bring about. Chapter 2 looks at how these markets work, both in theory and in practice.

Chapter 3 tells the story of tin. The rise of the mass-produced tin can at the beginning of this century created many fortunes. In 1974, as oil prices quadrupled, fears of raw material shortages helped push up the price of tin. At that time the subsequent world economic slump was not foreseen. The ITC based the floor price of the metal on these high prices; its intervention range (defined by the floor and ceiling price) was raised by 40 per cent in 1974. Many expected a return to high demand, and, rather than let the price fall when demand slackened, the ITC defended the floor price through the enforcing of export quotas and the building of a buffer stock. The price of tin in 1979 was double that of 1973.

By the 1980s, after the second oil price rise (of 1979) other commodity prices plummeted. This is, at the very least, a major reason why inflation has slowed down in the industrialised countries. Professor Wilfred Beckerman, an Oxford economist, has suggested that this is the entire reason for the slowdown in inflation. That is, the poor of the third world have paid for the solution to the economic problems of the rich, industrialised nations.

For more than ten years, the tin agreement was able to maintain the price of tin. Some commentators have seen this as the cause of the crash, saying that high tin prices discouraged demand for tin. In 1973 tin consumption reached its peak at 200,000 tonnes; by 1982 this had fallen to 140,000 tonnes. This view is far too simple. The period since 1973 has been one of massive technical change, accelerated by high energy prices. Tin's market position was eroded as other materials such as aluminium rose to challenge it. It is doubtful whether lower tin prices would have prevented such developments.

In the 1980s, a new producer, Brazil, opened low-cost tin mines. Cheap Brazilian tin would have undercut the tin market whatever the policies of the ITC. Brazil was not a member of the ITC, and between

---

The tin men

The traders of the London Metal Exchange usually spend most of the day in a state of controlled hysteria. Each of the seven metals bought and sold at the LME are traded in five-minute sessions, four times a day. The sessions start in silence, progress to a buzz as the clerks in the telephone booths behind the dealers take and pass on instructions from their offices, and rise to an ear-splitting crescendo during the last 15 seconds as bids and offers are made by open outcry. Men and women point, gesticulate, scream and shout across the ring to indicate their willingness to buy or sell.

Then, at 13.10 precisely, the howling stops, the dealers and clerks don their overcoats and make for the George and Vulture in Castle Court where, following in the footsteps of Charles Dickens and Mr Pickwick, they tuck into traditional fare: steak and kidney, spotted dick and roly-poly pudding.

The ritual has gone on almost unchanged since 1877 when a group of the leading metal merchants rented the upstairs room of a hatter's shop in Lombard Court, drew a chalk circle on the floor, and started shouting their wares.

The greatest risk they have run in the ensuing 108 years has been strained vocal chords.

Or so it seemed until the morning of Thursday October 24, when Pieter de Koning, the International Tin Council's buffer stock manager and the single biggest client in the tin market, placed a fateful call to the LME which brought tin trading shuddering to a standstill.

De Koning, an international civil servant whose job it is to ensure stability in the tin markets by buying and selling from an enormous stockpile of the metal owned by the International Tin Council — the 'club' of tin producers and consumers — had run out of money.

The announcement that he was broke caused near panic: ▶

1983 and 1986 it doubled its output of tin. Other producers, who were not members of the ITC or represented on it as producers, acted outside its production quotas. Britain, too, though a minor producer, doubled its tin production between 1980 and 1985. In the Far East, some producers whose countries were members of the ITC tried to evade ITC export controls by smuggling tin. Major tin producers did begin to adjust to the competition, substantially reducing output. This was, however, insufficient to prevent the build-up of surplus stocks. Nevertheless, the ITC continued to keep the tin price high by adding to its buffer stock. But underlying its efforts was the reality of an oversupplied market. The collapse of the ITC was, as one writer put it: 'the fuse which ignited a time bomb that had ticked away quietly under the tin world for nearly five years'.

- The London Metal Exchange, the world's pre-eminent metals market, halted all dealings in tin.
- Brokers and bankers who had extended credit to, or were owed money by, de Koning went into a spin.
- Governments of the big tin producing countries — Malaysia, Indonesia, Thailand, Bolivia and Brazil — scheduled emergency meetings. The question was: 'If the price collapses, what will happen to our economies?'
- Companies around the world started doing make-or-break arithmetic. If the crisis pushed prices below certain trigger points, they would go out of business. In the UK, the Cornwall tin mines are reckoned to be viable at a price of £6,500 to £7,000 a tonne. Anything below that would mean closure.

As the news broke, dealers rushed from the market, shell-shocked. 'I've never known a situation where nobody had any idea what on earth was going on,' says David Williamson, director of research for the trader Shearson Lehman Brothers, a subsidiary of American Express. 'Suddenly we were all looking at the whites of each other's eyes and wondering which ones may or may not be solvent. This was clearly what was going to happen so they closed the market.'

If they had not, everyone would have rushed into the market with their markers from the buffer stock manager.

'If a dozen banks and a dozen brokers all rush in and start selling collateral at once, what's the price going to do? Phut! There won't even be a market,' says Williamson.

Others were more phlegmatic. An accountant in one of the dealing firms did the only thing possible — he opened a book on the price at which tin would re-open when the market resumed.

The Sunday Times, 3 November 1985

Behind the events of October 1985 are these trends in tin production and consumption. The actual events, however, were triggered off by exchange rate fluctuations rather than these structural problems, as is explained in chapter 3. These fluctuations are a consequence of the instability of the financial world since the break-up of the Bretton Woods system. Some have claimed that LME metal traders should have foreseen the impending danger, but preferred instead to make profits from the existing situation. Ultimately, however, the City of London has lost a great deal from the crash, both in financial terms and in terms of confidence in the way the LME handles its business. Legal suits likely to last for years have been brought against the ITC, whose member governments refused to honour its debts. The million-dollar battles of banks and brokers to recover their money contrasts rather grotesquely with the struggles of impoverished miners to save their poorly paid and often highly dangerous jobs.

Bolivia's livelihood

For those countries whose economies are, for historical reasons, heavily dependent on one or two commodities, the story of tin is a reminder of their vulnerability. Chapter 4 looks at Bolivia and the role tin has played both past and present in its economy. Successive Bolivian governments have failed to prepare for the present crisis, although the uncompetitive position of Bolivian tin has been known for some time. At present, the Bolivian government seems ready to let the state mining industry die, whatever the cost to the mining communities.

Chapter 5 assesses whether there is any hope for the Bolivian tin industry, and looks at the wider implications for the economy and the people of Bolivia. The collapse of the tin market has provided those such as the World Bank, who have long argued that Bolivia's tin industry is in need of major restructuring, with an opportunity to implement some of their proposals. But the Bolivian people need a policy for rebuilding the country's productive base. Continued dependence on commodity exports is clearly not a solution. Bolivian history has been marked by the boom-bust cycles of such exports, first silver and now tin. At present, US troops have joined the Bolivian army to stamp out the only commodity, cocaine, which is today providing a means of survival for thousands of Bolivians. Alternatives are needed which will guarantee a future for Bolivia and the Bolivian people.

The final chapter draws together the many issues raised by the great tin crash. The case study used as an example is Bolivia, although people's lives have been ruined by the crash in a number of other countries. The tin crash is of very far-reaching significance. Today, the collapse of the tin agreement is being used to discredit commodity intervention agreements, in particular the idea that they should provide guaranteed income levels for the poorer producers. Commodity agreements are, however, sensible for both producers and consumers and still have a major role to play.

The story of tin is about the harsh realities of the present world economy. The laws of supply and demand allow only the strong and efficient to flourish. Social need and individual hardship are not a concern for those who believe there should be no interference in the market — unless, that is, powerful countervailing political forces are at work. In the case of Britain, for example, a Conservative government which had fought the coal miners for a year on the issue of the economic viability of pits, changed its stance when it came to the tin mines in Cornwall, where the Conservative Party is under challenge from the Liberal-Social Democrat Alliance.

For those who believe that social need should be a major consideration in policy, the story of tin offers a challenging dilemma. Rapid technological change and shifting patterns of production and consumption are part of the everyday reality of the world economy. How far the pace of change can be controlled to ease the painful process of transition to new economic activity is a major question of our times. Behind it lies a broader issue — the search for a more humane and democratic world economic order in which the weak are not forced to pay the cost of each new adjustment.

1 'Even the mice are leaving...'

'We housewives are desperate because we have nothing to take home. The *pulperias* [company shops] are empty; even the mice are leaving because there's no food. Our husbands are going to work on nothing. All we have to eat each day is bread and *sultana* water [a drink made with coffee bean husks]. Our children are falling asleep at the school desks because of empty stomachs. We have had to give them even less to eat. For example, if we have some bread rolls we have to share one between three or four of us and try to sell the rest to buy other foods such as vegetables and sugar. They don't kill us with bullets any longer but through hunger. Bullets would be preferable to this.'

Miner's wife from Siglo XX

Bolivia's tin miners are facing the gravest moment yet in the history of the mining communities. Long-term crisis in the mines combined with the collapse of the world tin market threatens the very future of tin in Bolivia. At stake too, is the future of the most combative workers in Bolivia and, some argue, in Latin America as a whole. The Bolivian miners have long challenged the country's political as well as economic order, taking on the army in many a bloody battle. The fate of tin is also the fate of their political project: a far-reaching transformation of Bolivia's economy and society towards the interests of the poor majority.

The Bolivian government, headed by the conservative politician, Victor Paz Estenssoro, came to office in August 1985 committed to 'shock treatment' to solve the country's financial crisis. Devaluation, a wage freeze and an end to subsidies on food and fuel paved the way for a deal with the International Monetary Fund (IMF), enabling the country to reschedule its debt. The collapse of the price of tin further reduced government revenue, creating even more difficulties for an already crisis-ridden economy. The government has announced the 'restructuring' of the state mining company, Comibol, with massive job losses.

The miners' traditional weapon for defending their rights, the strike, is no longer appropriate. The low price of tin has destroyed their bargaining power. Strike action only releases Comibol from obligations to pay wages and hastens the demise of the industry. The

14

miners have few weapons left to resist government policy, which since the austerity measures of August 1985 has fallen very heavily upon them.

The end of subsidised food, for instance, was a particularly hard blow for miners and their families. The government previously subsidised four basic products — meat, bread, sugar and rice — a subsidy which was worth between one-third and one-half of the miners' income. Without it, basic items of food are beyond the reach of most families. Although inflation has been reduced, the price index rose 174 per cent between August 1985 and August 1986. Some basic goods have risen even more; sugar went up 61 per cent between June and August 1986 and potatoes by 50 per cent.

Miners' wages were frozen at the equivalent of US$60 per month in August 1985; one year later they had fallen to US$43. Because their debts to the mining company are deducted each month, most miners have in fact received no cash wages for many months. These debts have accumulated, beginning with the change in salary levels in August 1985. Two advance payments were made at that time and a special Christmas payment was negotiated by the miners' union, all of which were subsequently deducted from wages. The cost of food bought at the company store is also deducted from wages and this has traditionally kept the miners in debt to the company.

However, cash alone would not solve the food problem in the

Impoverishment

Bolivia has consolidated its position as the poorest country in the western hemisphere with the exception of Haiti, with an infant mortality rate of at least 168 per thousand live births, half its children clinically malnourished (and 61 per cent suffering from goitre), real unemployment of between 40 and 50 per cent, and 60 per cent of a still predominantly rural population living well beneath the poverty line (infant mortality in the countryside is reliably assessed to be 210 per thousand live births). According to informal USAID estimates some 8 per cent of the population emigrated between 1982 and 1985, principally to neighbouring states. These new 'economic refugees' join approximately one million Bolivians — over one-sixth of the total population — working abroad. It can, therefore, be said without exaggeration that the great mass of Bolivians live in conditions more proximate to those in the Sahel than to those in Argentina; hunger and its related diseases are easily the single most important cause of death.

James Dunkerley, 'Bolivia at the crossroads', *Third World Quarterly*, January 1986

---

mining areas. With Comibol virtually bankrupt, the company stores have almost nothing to sell. A British aid worker visited the Catavi company store in March 1986 and found the shelves empty. 'The place echoes,' she writes, 'the women standing here tell us that there has been no bread for months. Many start to cry as they explain that their husbands have received only 'stars' [indicating a negative balance] on their payslips since October after all the deductions. Most leave with their shopping bags empty.'

Most families now have to live on one meal a day of bread, bean leaves and bean and potato peelings. They drink a tea made out of boiling coffee bean husk. Nutritional levels have fallen as people feel the effects of the poor diet. Poor living conditions have exacerbated the problem. The miners' houses, which belong to the company, are falling apart; rain leaks through the rooves.

The miners have had to pawn or sell their few possessions in order to survive. Some have sought temporary farm work at harvest time to supplement their incomes. Others have tried to grow their own food, planting beans on wasteground or in small plots on hills nearby. But most mines are at altitudes of 4,000 metres where very little grows. Mineral theft, *juqueo* as it is known, has increased as the struggle to survive has intensified, along with more serious forms of crime and delinquency.

The company hospital in Catavi has no medicines; it has been known to turn away women who have arrived to give birth and people have died from lack of attention. 'You die quicker in the hospital than at home', said a miner interviewed by a Bolivian human rights organisation. 'People no longer want to go into hospital because they've no confidence in it anymore. Specialists have left because Comibol offers such low salaries. There are no drugs and the only prescriptions given are for tranquillisers. Worst of all is the food, it consists of watery soup with a few noodles. The workers prefer home remedies to those of the hospital.'

For most of 1986 many miners, with broken helmets and worn out boots, continued to work despite their empty stomachs and the deteriorating conditions in the mines. They hoped to show that Comibol could be saved (see chapter 5). Comibol and the government, on the other hand, were preparing for closures. There was no investment in basic spare parts for machinery and frequent delays in supplying diesel to keep the mines working. The following report of conditions in Siglo XX appeared in the Bolivian newspaper, *Aqui* (3-9 May 1986):

> Seventy per cent of the engineering workshop is out of action for lack of spare parts. There are no tools nor the most basic materials. You only have to visit the tunnels in the Beza section or Block 4 to feel how unbreathable

the air is and fill your lungs with the thick dust which causes so much sickness in the mine.

'There is no air in here. A compressor has broken and there's no wire to repair the winding mechanism. Look at my mask. I only changed it a moment ago and it's already full of dust. The alarm isn't working. When we explode dynamite, we have to shout a warning... Apart from that, we don't have machines and tools. There are no spare parts.'

'What can we work with?' asked another miner. 'No brother, you cannot do with your hands what should be done by machines.' 'And you cannot work on an empty stomach', said another. 'Men are fainting in the mine with hunger. We don't have medicines for them and often there are no wagons to take them out of the mine. You just have to wait and let them recover by themselves... How can we produce without food?'

The labour force in the mines is now greatly reduced. Those over 60 were forced to retire early in 1986 and voluntary retirement offered to those between 50 and 55. Many married women employed by Comibol also lost their jobs, including doctors, nurses and teachers. Gradually, increasing numbers of miners, encouraged by government offers of redundancy pay, opted to leave the mines on their own accord. Morale became very low in the face of increasing hardship. 'The situation' a miner from Huanuni told a journalist in May, 'is desperate and disastrous, there is such total demoralisation amongst the workers that lately production has fallen 50 per cent.

Potosi — a tale of one city

'Just the announcement of mine closures is depopulating this city, pompously called the Monument of America.' These were the words of Luis Fernandez, President of the Civic Committee of Potosi, the world's highest town at 4,700 metres above sea level and one which is in danger of becoming a ghost town. He went on to say that in recent months over 250,000 people had left the Department of Potosi, the majority of whose inhabitants depend directly or indirectly on mining for survival.

Walking the streets there was a sense of a town dying. In marked contrast to the capital, La Paz, there were very few street sellers and those there were only sold cheap snacks. Few shops, or even the main market — usually a very busy place in Bolivian towns — seemed to have many customers. Looking at the people in the street I realised that there were plenty of elderly people and some children but very few 20-40 year olds. Houses have become incredibly cheap — the local joke is that they are the cheapest in the world — and the newspapers were full of advertisements for the auctions of house contents. I sat in a milk bar for an hour one afternoon, and in that time only one other person came in, to buy a litre of milk, but walked out again in disgust when he was told the price. ▶

It is not just the depopulation of the city that hits you, but the grinding poverty of those who are still there, both those in work and the unemployed. For a 48 hour week the miners of Potosi earn between $US20 and 40 per month, which makes things like the price of milk very important. The harshness of daily life was obvious and the resentment at what was really happening to Potosi was clearly voiced by everyone I spoke to. Nowhere was this more strongly expressed than on 6th August, Bolivia's national day.

In Potosi's main square at about 3 pm that day the sounds of a traditional (since colonial times) Bolivian brass band heralded the start of the annual civic parade. What was unusual about the parade was that as well as various patriotic banners and flags, virtually all the groups who filed past in the course of about an hour — school and university students, traders, co-operatives, miners and women's groups — had banners protesting in strong terms at the mine closures, government economic policy and US imperialism...

The grim reality of life for those without regular work was matched by the appalling pay and conditions of those miners who still had a job (one of Potosi's main mines employed 2,300 a year ago and now employs only 1,300). At the entrance to the Pailaviri mine, one of Potosi's largest, stands a COMIBOL notice which bears the legend: 'In order to be here tomorrow, work safely today.' Carefully avoiding the high tension cable which runs at head height, I walked through water past the icicles hanging from the walls of the mine tunnel beyond the entrance. Within a few hundred metres the temperature had risen considerably. The guide told me that at the mining face the temperature reaches 40 degrees centigrade and the miners often work naked. The pneumatic drills they support with their bodies weigh between 26 and 36 kilos.

In the Pailaviri mine there are 14 levels still being worked (3 more are now flooded) each separated by about 30 metres of rock. Serious and fatal accidents are common, often due to the collapse of tunnels during exploration for fresh seams of lead and silver. Silicosis is common, but miners receive no ill health pension unless they are officially certified as being 90 per cent disabled as a result of the disease.

The mood in Potosi was perhaps best summed up by part of an advertisement placed in a local newspaper by the Tomas Frias University to mark Bolivia's national day, which said: 'Potosi has given everything to the Fatherland and for the Fatherland. It is time that the Fatherland did something to stop Potosi dying.'

Roy Youdale, December 1986

By August 1986, the total workforce had fallen to 19,000. One-third of Comibol's workforce had either left or been removed from their jobs. By the end of the year an estimated 18,500 Comibol miners and other personnel had handed in their voluntary resignations. Priority has been given to funding redundancy payments. As Comibol has no funds for such purposes, money has been taken out of the 'Social Emergency Fund' created with support from the United Nations and originally intended to generate new sources of employment through reactivating the productive sectors of the economy. In September, the government proposed putting more funds into the redundancy programme, but the FSTMB rejected its offer. Many miners went on hunger strike in a bid to secure a better deal. Agreement was reached between the FSTMB and the government in January 1987. Workers dismissed since the 1985 tin crash will receive US$35 for every year they have worked in the state mining industry (the miners had demanded US$750). There would also be bonus payments of US$1,500 to help miners 'relocate'. These figures are grossly inadequate for miners who have given years of service to Comibol and will do little to ease the misery of those losing their livelihoods (see box below). Many still doubt the ability of the government to find the redundancy money they have promised.

The future for miners who leave their jobs is bleak. Redundancy payments will only pay off debts or buy a few basic necessities. When

---

Relocation

The Espinoza family arrived at Río Seco last July after receiving separation pay amounting to $1,500 in compensation for 18 years of work in the Matilde mine. Guillermina Epinoza, her spouse and five children had been given three weeks to vacate their home and leave the mining town in one of 15 trucks that took families away that day. 'Our leave-taking was very painful,' recalls Guillermina. 'They came and told us to grab our things and climb aboard the waiting truck. We wept as we left. I had really been at home at the mine. When they moved me, I felt — I don't know — that I'd left some part of me there.'

The Espinozas moved to Río Seco, where 50 workers from Matilde had bought land years before. A house was still being built and they had to roof it quickly, which took a substantial portion of their separation pay. They have no running water or electricity.

Other 'relocated' mining families have had to rent or share dwellings with other families. According to a recent census in the city of Cochabamba, three-fourths of the 945 former miners who were relocated there did not have their own homes. Only 3.2 per cent had received all the severance benefits promised by the government.

▶

Like most former miners, Guillermina's spouse has not found work here in La Paz because of increased competition for few jobs. Most ex-miners do not have the skills needed for industrial jobs. Furthermore, their reputation as 'agitators' has closed many doors to them. 'They seem to be afraid of us,' said a woman who had recently arrived from the mines.

Far from finding support and solidarity among urban workers, mining families are running into indifference and often outright rejection. The law of the jungle reigns in the cities, where the new influx of migrants represents an additional pressure on scarce income sources and social services. 'Why didn't they stay where they were? Why didn't they stay where they were? Why have they come here?' complained vendors at one of the capital's open air markets as a woman from one mine tried to set up a juice stand.

'They told me the market was only for people from here and kicked me out,' the newcomer said.

Besides housing shortages and unemployment, the former miners are worried about their children's health and educational needs. Many children have gotten sick because of the change in climate, and some, already weakened by malnutrition, have died. Many lost a school year because they had to leave the mine at mid-term. Local school systems are having trouble absorbing the estimated 79,000 new arrivals.

Latinamerica Press, 12 February 1987

the miners leave the mines, they must also leave their company house and their children must leave the company school. There are few prospects of work in Bolivia for a redundant miner. The Central Bank put unemployment at 20 per cent at the end of 1985. The COB estimated that open unemployment for 1986 will be nearly 30 per cent. Others suggest that real unemployment may be as high as 50 per cent. A total of 30,000 workers (including 8,000 Comibol employees) lost their jobs between August 1985 and August 1986. Most of these people will join the thousands of Bolivians who today live in conditions of absolute poverty (see box on page 15).

The government talks of 'relocating' miners who have lost their jobs, which means finding them work in other mining ventures or in colonisation programmes in tropical areas. However, no colonisation schemes have actually been implemented. Much infrastructural investment would be needed to provide services for the people in the areas concerned. A miner from Siglo XX described his situation:

What are those of us who leave going to live off in the towns? Our redundancy money won't last long. Our only option is processing cocaine

Doped economy

Truckloads of unemployed miners from Bolivia's highlands are heading for the subtropical Chapare plains in a modern version of the gold rush. Hard months await them in this hostile new environment while they clear land to plant the bush which has become the mainstay of Bolivia's 'parallel economy': coca.

For centuries, the Quechua and Aymara peoples have used the coca leaf for medicine, ritual and to stave off hunger. But international demand for cocaine has transformed it into a valuable raw material whose influence has penetrated all levels of Bolivian society...

Bolivia's traditional coca-growing region is in the warm Yungas valleys north-east of La Paz. A hardy bush which can thrive in poor soils, coca yields four harvests a year of leaves which are easy to carry, a boon in isolated rural areas where transportation is scarce. In recent years, vast areas have been planted with coca in the Chapare lowlands which now produce 80 per cent of Bolivian cocaine and 40-45 per cent of the supply for the world market.

Although the coca boom has meant sudden wealth for many, the farmers who grow the bush continue to live in impoverished surroundings. Narrow dirt roads lead to adobe shacks without water or electricity which may have new pick-up trucks parked outside but which house ragged, anaemic children who have no access to schooling or health care...

The Chapare is a lawless territory where the drug mafia operates well-armed security systems to protect its interests. The traffickers get advance warning by radio of the raids periodically carried out by the armed forces and the 'Leopards', the US-funded narcotics force notorious for its corruption and the extortionate tactics it uses against the local population...

'The economy is doped', says Bolivian economist Alvar Moscoso. 'Drug trafficking harms it, but it needs it to survive.' The cost of this addiction: staple food crops are being neglected, national industry cannot compete with the flood of imports bought with 'coca-dollars' and the influence of the trades unions is being eroded as more and more workers are forced to seek a living outside the productive sector.

Bolivia Bulletin, La Paz, Bolivia, July 1986

paste and perhaps gold mining, but without any of the basic services we are used to, such as health care and education. None of us have our own houses, and the company will throw us out. We only have a few belongings and some of these are pawned.

Some of the miners have headed for the towns, some back to the countryside around the north of Potosi and Cochabamba from where many of them originate and still have relatives. Others have headed for Chapare, seeking work treading coca leaves (see box on page 21). Many, such as this miner from Huanuni, are leaving the country:

There's no point in staying in the mines any longer. The government has stopped all subsidies in the *pulperias*, frozen our wages and restricted overtime. I'm also going to leave, but I shall go very far away where there are better standards of living and more jobs, like Argentina. Two weeks ago, nine families from Huanuni went there. Because in our country there are no guarantees of anything, and the future is very uncertain.

Potosí

2 How mineral commodity markets work

The following describes the visit of a Bolivian miner, Higon Cussi, to London:

His first London visit is to the place where the permanent link between Bolivia's poverty and our wealth is forged — on the floor of the London Metal Exchange...

Higon is amazed. He can't see any tin. 'I imagined that they would show samples — not that they would just do it by talking.'

Christopher Green... a director of the London Metal Exchange, explains to him just how it works. 'Instead of passing over pieces of metal we pass over pieces of paper. These are documents of title to tin which is kept in warehouses.'

'But all this shouting about prices', says Higon, 'takes no account of the human effort which goes into the production of the metal.'

'The price is determined by the international conjunction of supply and demand', explains Green kindly. 'Members here will be aware of the hardship that goes into the production of tin. But this market is just one process in the long chain of bringing metal to where it is needed.'

'I still think that the human contribution should be given more importance, so that the workers are given a fairer price.'

'That doesn't come into the calculation of the price. This is made by the international conditions ruling in the tin market overall.'

New Internationalist, January 1984

Mineral commodities, of which tin is an example, are produced in widely differing countries all over the world. At one end of the scale is the rich USA, a producer of many minerals, which has been extensively explored for new and cheaper supplies. There, production takes place using the most modern methods and workers are well paid, by international standards. Communications are good and machinery and energy sources are readily available. Workers have access to a plentiful supply of consumer goods.

At the other end are the poor countries of the third world, in particular those who are heavily dependent on the foreign exchange earnings from a single mineral product — such as bauxite, which is used to produce aluminium or, in the case of Bolivia until recently, tin. Although in some places the most modern technology is imported, in general conditions are very different from those in North American mining. One striking result is that workers mining the same metal can have hugely different standards of living. Cornish tin miners, for instance, earn far more than those in Bolivia. Both, however, are at the mercy of the world tin crisis.

The crash of the tin market is creating human tragedies around the globe and nowhere more so than in Bolivia. Behind this crash are apparently 'impersonal' market forces, whose victims, however, are amongst the poorest countries and the most impoverished of the world's workers.

The nature of these 'impersonal' forces is not obvious to anybody outside the specialised world of metals. Easily visible phenomena such as the London Metal Exchange, volatile prices and a general idea of supply and demand by no means tell the whole story. Behind them is a complex system of interactions. These include, for instance, the geological conditions in every mine and the variety of possible mining methods for individual mines, each with a different cost and yield. Similarly, there are a wide range of uses for the mineral, again with a variety of techniques and possibilities of substitution of one material by another. This complex system is barely comprehensible even to full-time market analysts. This is because the market is not specifically the physical place of the London Metal Exchange or even the internationally linked groups of traders and brokers. The market is the whole network of underlying technical factors and all the people making local decisions in relation to them.

Free market economists argue that individual producers or consumers do not need to understand all this. It is only necessary that all producers know their own costs of production (or, for consumers, how much they have to spend) and the price which the market determines. The rest of the information has been distilled from the network of interactions into one number: the price. For such economists, it is impossible to design a better system. If change occurs, either it will do so smoothly (if everyone behaves normally) or, if there are sudden changes, then it is best to leave well alone and let the market do the organising.

This view ignores the fundamental nature of capitalism: an urge to change which was unknown in any previous economic system. By forever revolutionising the means and methods of production, capitalism seeks constantly to expand. Each individual entrepreneur in search of higher profits provides a small part of an overall dynamic. The application of scientific knowledge and techniques and the constant reorganisation of economic life are fundamental. Booms and slumps — sudden changes — are an accompanying feature of the system.

24

The Ring of the London Metal Exchange: Dealings are conducted orally by ring-dealing firms whose representatives make bids and offers to each other across the Ring. A deal is immediately concluded when a bid or offer is accepted. Contracts between the firms concerned will be exchanged before noon the following day. Each metal is traded separately in five minute rings of which there are two in each session, and two sessions per day

London Metal Exchange

25

At the London Metal Exchange metal dealers meet to buy and sell, in order to make a profit. Young brokers earn high salaries (as much as £40,000 per year) for work which affects the livelihoods of thousands of people far away. The successful brokerage firm can expect to make millions

Philip Wolmuth

26

In mineral commodity markets, for example, change is built into the process in a very fundamental way. Old mines become exhausted or their production costs rise as more difficult geological conditions are encountered. New technology, economic recession and shifting patterns of consumption all change demand. The costs of adjusting to these uncoordinated changes are left to lie where they fall, and are usually borne by the weakest in society. The system is fundamentally wasteful of the resource which lies at its very foundation: human beings.

This chapter looks in detail at how mineral commodity markets work so that the tin market and the causes of the crash can be understood. First, it covers the system of production and sale of minerals in what could be called 'normal' conditions (ie how it should work according to the logic of the free market economists) and, more importantly, how this system deals with change. Second, it looks more closely at the system as it operates in practice, the uncertainties which are built into it and the need for intervention in the market.

The simple view

In theory, prices of metals depend upon the balance of supply and demand in the world market, but what is meant by the term 'world market' differs considerably from metal to metal. For some metals the majority of trading takes the form of long-term supply contracts between the mine's owners and the puchaser who will use the metal. This is typical, for instance in the case of uranium, where only a small portion is traded through intermediary agents. In this situation the metal being shipped from the mine can be at a price agreed years earlier, and there is no single price for the whole market — each shipment depends on these individual contracts of varying ages and a single mine may be producing to meet a number of contracts at the same time. This suits the purchaser who knows well in advance what the material is going to cost and who is ensured of security of supply.

For other metals — copper, zinc, lead, silver, aluminium, nickel and, until the crash, tin — there is an elaborate system of trading, with buyers and sellers interacting to set the market price. These metals are traded across the floor of the London Metal Exchange and prices depend on bids and offers in this concrete marketplace.

At the LME metal dealers meet to buy and sell, in order to make a profit. Ultimately they act as middlemen or agents between the two sides of the market. It is a noisy market where young men and a few women working for firms of metal brokers (sometimes owned by large financial conglomerates) shout bids and offers for the delivery of metals at various prices. A good comparison might be with a wholesale fruit market although much larger sums of money are at stake. These young brokers earn high salaries (as much as £40,000 per year) for work which affects the livelihoods of thousands of people far away. The successful brokerage firm can expect to make millions.

The London Metal Exchange

Before the crash there were three markets for tin: New York; Penang, a purely physical market where the commodity itself is bought by traders and consumers; and the London Metal Exchange, where trading consists largely of futures (in recent years physical trading of tin has accounted for only about one-fifth of LME business). To understand the events surrounding the 'Great Tin Crash', it is important to clarify the role of the LME, the world's biggest and oldest metals market.

The LME was founded in 1877 and dominated trading in non-ferrous metals as a result of the pre-eminence of British manufacturing. London was at this time the ackowledged commercial and financial centre of the world. Although Britain's commercial supremacy began to decline shortly after the turn of the century, the LME retained its control over world metal markets. This was especially so in the case of tin because tin production and smelting remained in British hands. Also the convenience of the LME for merchants and financiers was well established and outweighed the fact that the UK was no longer the main market.

Organised commodity markets such as the LME evolved to provide traders with a number of safeguards, of which greater protection from adverse price fluctuations is just one. If no market existed at all, industrial consumers needing tin would have to find an individual supplier with whom to negotiate a price. In the absence of a market there are limited opportunities for consumers to find out whether cheaper alternatives exist, whether the supply is expensive or not, or to ensure additional supplies if the first source becomes unavailable (because of mining disasters, strikes, wars, and so on). Similarly, the existence of a market ensures that producers are not dependent on a single consumer who might go broke or not take the material for some other reason.

With the existence of a market, price dispersion narrows sharply and the probability of actually making a successful sale or purchase is increased. Instead of paying a different price to each mine owner there is a single price for all tin of a given type and quality, no matter what the source. The price which both producers and consumers have to take into account is known to everyone. Regular supplies from a wide variety of sources ensure supplies are forthcoming even if one mine fails while, at the same time, suppliers know they can find a market for their product. ▶

Large-scale industry requires planning. Giant furnaces and smelters cannot be shut down, or production lines stopped, because of temporary shortages of metal input. To ensure that a continuous supply is maintained, it is possible to build up stocks. However, an alternative is to enter into a contract for tin to be delivered in, say, nine months' time. The purchaser has then secured a supply, but the market price at the time the contract was made (ie the 'spot' price for immediate delivery) may be higher or lower than the price paid for the contract. This, together with the ability to sell these contracts to third parties, contains the seeds of speculation which can sometimes turn the LME into a gambling house.

Speculators make extensive use of the LME to profit from accurate forecasting of the fluctuations of metal prices without any obligation to take or make delivery. The 10 per cent deposit system means they can double their money if the market fluctuates 10 per cent in their favour, or lose it all if it moves 10 per cent against. Such activities are justified by some because they help 'broaden' the market through a willingness to accept risks, and this facilitates hedging operations. Without them, it is argued, there would be a shortage of risk capital and the market would lack the liquidity to function smoothly.

Speculation is carried out by some august people. John Maynard Keynes, the father of post-war economics, is said to have been found measuring the chapel of King's College, Cambridge, when he thought he might have to take actual delivery of metal he had speculated on. The hope of all speculators is to be able to corner the market — to hold a sufficiently large share of the product to be able to dictate the price and then sell on one's own terms at a huge profit. Keynes is said to have done this. More recently the oil rich Hunt brothers attempted to corner the silver market and literally lost a fortune when they failed. Apart from cornering the market, it is possible to make large, if more modest profits, in both a rising and, more surprisingly, a falling market. In the first case a purchase is made and then sold at the higher price to give a straight profit. In the second, metal holders first sell and then buy back the material at a cheaper price. They then hold their original stock of material plus the cash difference between the selling and rebuying price.

Critics allege that the LME encourages price instability because it attracts such a volume of speculative activity. Many price movements on the LME, especially very short-term ones, are not justified by supply and demand conditions, and speculative activity has accounted for some of these. Tin in particular, as a high-value commodity, has attracted speculative activity in conditions of inflation and currency instability. The volatility of the LME is illustrated by the events of June 1979. The LME price for tin

▶

fluctuated just under 10 per cent; the trough and peak were reached in just a few days. The range on the Penang market, however, was only 0.5 per cent and on the New York market, under 3 per cent.

Nevertheless, the most powerful factor influencing raw material prices is the international economic cycle, particularly in today's interdependent world economy. Economic recession, for example, has a much greater influence on commodity prices than anything else. In the 1980s recession has drastically cut demand for mineral commodities and prices have plummeted. Other factors such as inflation, political instability, cartels, natural disasters and buffer stock operations also influence prices.

The LME attracts considerable speculative activity; dealers operate in the market to make quick profits either for themselves or for their speculating clients (see page 28). From time to time the activities of these 'market makers' can affect the whole system of production and consumption, causing temporary wild fluctuations in prices not justified by basic changes in supply and demand. However, most of the time they and the market are in the grip of the more fundamental and powerful forces discussed below.

Demand in the market is governed by the needs of those using the metal in industry. They decide how much they are prepared to buy at any given price in relation to how much is needed in their production process and, eventually, in relation to what their customers are prepared to pay for those products. Conversely, supply is related to how much mine owners can increase output and to their costs of production. If the tin price falls below their costs they cannot sell at a profit and they will reduce supply. These underlying conditions of supply and demand ultimately govern the prices at which metal commodities are traded, however frenetic the buying and selling and however much the prices fluctuate.

The result of the public trading of metals at the LME is that the prices at which goods are being traded are more clearly known to third parties than in the long-term trading relationships (where only each buyer and seller know the price they have agreed). However, producers never know very far ahead of time what the price will be, although both they and industrial consumers would generally prefer to know in advance. The consumers need to know what their costs will be when making decisions affecting the future of their own business (eg whether to buy new furnaces or machinery, or whether to plan a new product line dependent on the supply of materials), and producers need to know whether it is worthwhile bringing a new mine facility into being, whether they can afford to agree to a pay rise, and so on. For markets such as tin, the producers do not have the fallback of long-term contracts with guaranteed prices. There is much uncertainty even in normal times.

While supply and demand are the mechanisms by which prices are set, they do little to explain why the miner in the third world is so badly off compared to the consumer in the industrialised nations. The answers given to Higon Cussi contain no real explanation. To understand why he gets so little for his labour in producing the commodity, while the products of the richer nations are so expensive (the so-called 'terms of trade'), it is necessary to look beyond the operation of markets to the world distribution of economic, political and, ulimately, military power.

The supply side

Mineral commodities are produced by a surprising variety of mining methods, ranging from the deep mining of ores to open pits, leaching by chemical solutions and processing of sediments. At any particular time all these methods may be in operation around the world, as is the case with tin. The costs of each method and each individual mine will vary according to the mine's remoteness, the levels of mechanisation, and the use of labour and other inputs. Furthermore, each mine has different geological conditions and grades of ore.

Mines can therefore be ranked according to costs of production methods and consequent profitability for the owners. At any given level of market prices this scale of costs of production would show the profitability of any particular mine. Any mine with costs above the market price would go out of business; those with costs exactly equal to the price will yield no profit; while those with costs below will show profits for the owner — the so-called 'producer's surplus'. The owner with the cheapest and easiest to operate mines makes the biggest profits. As this profit is largely dependent upon the variability of natural conditions and the good fortune to have accessible ores, rather than upon the skills and hard work of the mine's owners, governments frequently attempt to tax away these excess profits in the form of 'royalties' and other taxes. The benefits, the 'economic rents', are then shared amongst the nation's population at large.

The demand side

Demand for mineral commodities is affected by developments anywhere along the line from the smelters to the final use of the material. However, the person who buys a new hi-fi doesn't think

31

about the solder inside the machine. Instead, his or her decision to buy a particular item depends on a whole host of factors, including price, but also the technical developments which create new products and change old ones.

The complexity of the processes affecting demand in the market can be illustrated by two phenomena. One is the rise in ownership of consumer durables. Typically a new product, such as a television set, appears and is obtained by a few people. Then ownership becomes more widespread until the market is saturated — for example, perhaps 95 per cent for televisions but less than 50 per cent for freezers in the UK where houses are small. While the big surge in ownership is taking place, the demand for parts and components for the product, and consequently for metals, glass and so on, is at a peak. After saturation levels are reached, however, demand weakens until it just covers replacement of old machines. In some cases the arrival of a new product can involve other knock-on effects. The development of television has led to declining cinema attendance; ownership of refrigerators and freezers opens up the world of frozen food and excludes older methods, such as the tin can, of preserving and distributing food.

A second example involves the unforeseen effects which can result from substitution. The concept of substitution dominates current economic theory. How far is it possible to replace one good by another? In consumption, people may switch to wheat instead of maize as they grow wealthier or as wheat becomes cheaper; in production, a machine may replace a number of workers. Mineral commodities are generally used as inputs to some other production process, for example metal smelting and processing, which are in turn used in some other product. The possibility exists for both consumer and manufacturer substitution. Manufacturers can replace one metal by another in their goods (just as they might replace oil by gas as their source of energy) and consumers can turn, for instance, from a brass to a steel product, or even replace a metal by wood or plastic. The choices involved depend on relative prices and the technical possibility of substituting one material for another.

Because it is *relative* prices which count, demand can drop without any changes in the costs and conditions of supply of a commodity, because of changes in the costs and prices of the substitutes. The increase in the demand for nuclear power in the 1970s did not take place because nuclear power became cheaper but because the alternative, oil, became expensive.

Yet another complication is the following. An example of substitution on the production side in response to price shifts is what happened following the steep rise in energy prices in 1973-74. The price rise encouraged energy-saving technologies involving less heat, and led to a shift away from those materials requiring heat in processing. People substituted away from energy. But the rise in energy prices also had big and deleterious effect on those other products and goods which required energy in production (its 'complements', in economic jargon). It is not only the increasing price of a mineral itself which can lead to a reduction in its use, but also changes in prices of complements and an increasing pace of technical change. Substitution can thus have not only direct effects, one good for another, but also knock-on effects through the associated complements.

Interpreting the events of the 1970s is therefore very difficult. It is not easy to sort out the impacts of higher energy prices, the fall in demand as recession and more conservative economic policies followed, and rising and then falling prices for substitutes and complements. Those who blame low demand for commodities such as tin on high prices are therefore simplifying a very complex process.

Adjusting to change

What happens when there are changes in the supply and demand balance? Demand might change for technical reasons: for example a new use for tin or a big change in the costs of alternative and competing products. Supply might change if a major new source were found or another cut off. Either way the impact on the mining industry can be assessed firstly by looking at the supply-demand balance in the new situation. Once a price is set, the list which ranks all the world's mines by their cost category will indicate who can stay in operation. The cheapest mines will stay in existence as will those whose costs exactly equal the market price. *All other mines with costs higher than this should cease production.*

In theory, as demand falls or as a new source of cheaper supply comes into being, an individual mine (the marginal mine) would go out of production. The change would be smooth and affect only a relatively small number of people, although the hardship for them is no less real. There is no large-scale closure of mines, with effects big enough to cripple an entire economy.

This is how the market 'normally' operates in theory. The most striking aspect of the theory is that it is completely impersonal. As human and social costs are not usually counted by the market, the costs of adjustment to a changed situation are not distributed in any fair way; they fall on whoever is weakest or unlucky. The gains of switching to alternative methods of production using cheaper techniques or materials are made by the big firms who make more profits, and by

33

their customers who have cheaper goods.

Some writers have seen this as the source of capitalism's dynamism; a pool of wealth is made available to reinvest and bring about more changes. To endanger it by sharing the costs of change, they argue, would spread the benefits of change more thinly and inhibit change itself. It is certainly true that maintaining technical change requires constant high levels of investment in new capital goods and techniques, whether under capitalism or communism. The resources for this investment can, however, be generated by technical and scientific innovation — an increase in the whole of society's productive power — instead of by merely redistributing wealth from one group of producers or consumers to another.

Closer to reality

Mineral commodity prices are not really determined in the relatively simple way described above. The production of metal commodities from deep mines involves particularly complex technical and economic considerations. To open up a new deep mine requires a large investment and it may take years to bring it to the point of production. If the mine is to be in an inhospitable location it may need the supply of communications (road or rail, telephones and so on), water and all the necessities of life for those who are going to work there. Before beginning, the mine operator will want to know that the product can be sold profitably, which means taking a view of future needs for the product over the whole life of the mine. As has been explained, the market for tin is uncertain. On the other hand, once a mine is in existence it will not easily go out of production as long as the price of the output can cover wages and other running costs. The operation stays in existence even though the owners cannot recover the initial capital investments. In addition, there are many different ways to operate an existing mine. In hard times a mine manager may go for 'high grading', taking only the very best part of the ore, but when prices are high it may be worthwhile reprocessing the 'tailings', the waste from a previous extraction process. A mine which is uneconomic on its track record in one form of operation may become profitable if operated in a different way.

The simple view of 'normal' market operations is now beginning to blur. Ranking mines by cost becomes more difficult in practice, as costs are not as clearly defined as they might appear.

Exploration for new resources is continually being carried out because if a cheaper source is found it will provide larger profit margins than existing mines. The theory suggests that the new resources would

34

replace an older source. However, mining operations never run as smoothly as this. Instead, mine managers struggle to keep their own mines viable by changing mining tactics and hanging on in case survival should turn out to be possible. The problem is that very often the appropriate responses are not clear cut and managers cannot always distinguish a 'bad patch' in the market from one requiring more fundamental adjustment. Even if it becomes obvious that such adjustment is necessary, it is still unclear which mines are the candidates for extinction — the so-called marginal mines. This is the situation for tin at present.

Instabilities

The operation of mineral commodity markets is, therefore, far from smooth. Large-scale investments are made on the basis of expectations which may turn out to be false. Instead, the market develops in swings, with great exploration booms when high prices and profits are expected and large investments are made in new mines. The greatest recent example of this was the wide number of projects approved in the 1970s when a resumption of world economic growth was widely expected. These have come to fruition in a period of recession, with its overcrowded markets, and have added to the difficulties of suppliers.

Although world economic growth is now on the upturn, there is no sign of a return to the era following the Second World War when international trade expanded dramatically and exchange rates were stabilised in the Bretton Woods Agreement.

Even if the market could operate in the simple 'normal' mode outlined at the beginning of this chapter, prices would still fluctuate as new supplies were found and old ones used up, or when the final uses of the product shifted as technology progressed and world consumption patterns changed. The complexities of mineral exploration and uncertainty of future markets mean that prices are likely to be unstable and that there will be inequalities between supply and demand. In these circumstances, we can expect to see periods when prices are high and shortages exist, and others when low prices are accompanied by shut-downs of production. For these reasons both consuming and producing nations have sought to protect themselves in a number of ways.

Stabilisation mechanisms

Various efforts have been made to lessen the damage caused by the unpredictability of the system. These often take the form of commodity agreements such as the ITA, which establish mechanisms for intervening in the market. This usually means setting up a body which will act as a market stabiliser by guaranteeing limits within which prices can move. If prices rise above a certain level the body acts to increase supply by selling material from a stockpile. If prices go below a lower limit, demand is increased by buying for the stockpile. This requires the establishment and financing of a stockpile by producer groups, consumers or both.

Sometimes, however, the stockpile fails. It may be exhausted in periods of extended shortage or, as is now the case with tin, may grow so big that to continue funding it becomes very difficult and it is replaced by production quotas. For tin, both price intervention and quotas were needed (see box on page 46).

To the free market economist the existence of such an intervention mechanism is highly suspect. They fear it will lead to cartel arrangements which limit supplies in order to drive up prices and result in transfers to producers which would not occur in the 'free' market. The last tin agreement was influenced by the United Nations Conference on Trade and Development (UNCTAD) which saw commodity agreements as a useful method of transferring resources from the rich industrialised countries to the poorer third world. But the ITA is not comparable to OPEC. In contrast to OPEC, the tin producers have not had the power to enforce such high prices. Both tin producers and consumers are represented on the ITC, with votes distributed in proportion to a country's consumption or production and a two-thirds majority required to pass a motion. No 'TINPEC' has ever existed.

Although there are positive aspects about such commodity agreements, they cannot give complete protection to those involved in producing materials. Responsibilty for what happens at a national level when changes in prices and/or demand for minerals occur lies with the governments of producing countries. But their capacity to respond is not equal; nations such as Bolivia do not have the same means to deal with problems as the USA or a Western European state. Whereas the British government can easily afford to subsidise its tin industry, Bolivia cannot.

The fictional idea of equality between producers and consumers, or between mine owner and miner, leads to a position of non-intervention; ie that the costs should be left to lie where they fall. The benefits of changes in technology and the use of new materials are felt mainly in the rich consumer countries. The costs of those changes are felt most by the poorest countries who lack the diversified economic structures which could cushion a collapse of one sector of activity.

The impact of a crash

Without stabilisation mechanisms the market would impose its harsh logic from time to time, with erratic tin prices, and closures hitting the most expensive mines. There would be booms and crashes, causing great hardship. But when an intervention agreement collapses the situation is even more catastrophic. Such a crash leads to even faster and larger closures. Workers lose their jobs and incomes. As their spending falls, knock-on effects reverberate through the economy causing others to be thrown out of work; there is a general lowering of living standards. Governments lose the tax revenues which finance government spending and social programmes. In addition, the loss of foreign exchange earnings hits the economy in a general way, forcing shifts in currency values and restricting the ability to import foreign goods. Thus the impact of a crisis not only affects the workers directly concerned, but has consequences for the nation as a whole.

These consequences are, of course, much more serious for third world countries with limited alternatives. In Britain the end of tin production is a blow for the workers concerned and has a devastating regional impact on the Cornish economy, but the economy as a whole is sufficiently large and diversified to absorb the effects. The reverse is true for Bolivia. The lesson is not that commodity agreements are harmful, as the free market economists argue, but that they must be given the means to work effectively. Only the rich consumer nations have the economic capacity to guarantee this.

3 The story of tin

The tin market is going through a period of profound structural change. Adjustments which should have taken years are taking place in months. Yet in the two years prior to the tin crash, production and consumption of tin were broadly in balance. In fact, there was a small shortfall of production when additional consumption had to be met from stocks. Why did the tin market collapse at a time when production was well matched to consumption?

To answer this question, this chapter traces the story of tin. It begins by looking at: Who produces tin and in what ways? Who consumes it and what is it used for? These questions, or the supply and demand sides of the tin market, provide a key to current events and future possibilities.

The supply side

Chart (a) on page 39 shows which countries produced tin in 1981 and the methods used. It also gives an estimate of the costs for each of these and indicates which are the cheaper and the most expensive producers. Bolivia is the highest-cost producer, although this is due in part to the strength of the peso over that period.

Production levels of tin in 1970 and 1985 are shown in chart (b). The most significant feature is the growth in production from new sources, in particular from Brazil. In 1981 the Brazilian government took measures to transform the country's tin industry. At that time tin was mostly produced by independent miners working small areas and using very primitive techniques. Anxious to deal with its trade deficit, the government implemented a US$13 billion ten-year development plan for the non-ferrous minerals sector, focusing on development in the remote Amazon Basin. Here, the Paranapanema company, which had previously mined tin in Rondonia, discovered rich alluvial cassiterite deposits and turned them into some of the richest tin mines in the world. Reserves at the Pitinga mining complex are reported to be sufficient for nearly thirty years' production at a rate of 20,000 tonnes of tin per year. Although a considerable initial investment in infrastructure was required, mining costs are very low, estimated at only £2,500 a tonne. At those costs Paranapanema is one of the few tin producers with a certain future, well able to survive the fall in tin prices. Brazil is set to replace Malaysia as the world's leading tin producer.

No other mines in the world can match Pitinga's low costs. Different mining techniques involve different costs. Tin in Southeast Asia is

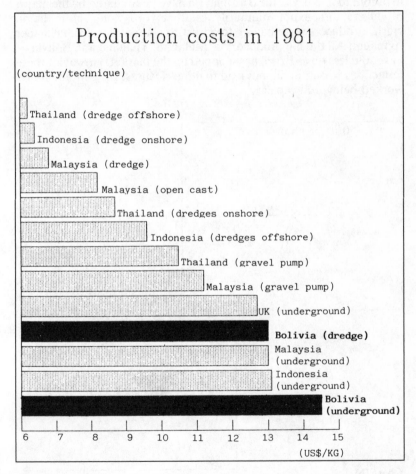

Chart (a)

Bolivian tin from underground mines was the most expensive in the world in 1981. Although this was due in part to the overvaluation of the currency, even adjusting for this, Bolivian tin is still amongst the most expensive.
Source: *International Tin Council.*

usually produced by dredging or gravel pumping, while in Bolivia it is deep mined. The deep mining system generally means higher costs, as chart (a) indicates, and is even more vulnerable to the pressures of oversupply. The problems of Bolivian mines are examined further in chapter 3.

If demand were static, the cheaper Brazilian tin would force the more expensive tin off the market. Chart (b) shows that the reductions in output to make way for Brazilian tin have been shared by the major producers, though not voluntarily. In other words, long before the tin crash, producers were having to adjust to competition from cheaper suppliers. All the big producers — Malaysia, Thailand and Bolivia — have sold less tin as Brazil has scooped up the market. However, these reductions in output did not lead to mine closures. Instead, the mines worked below full capacity.

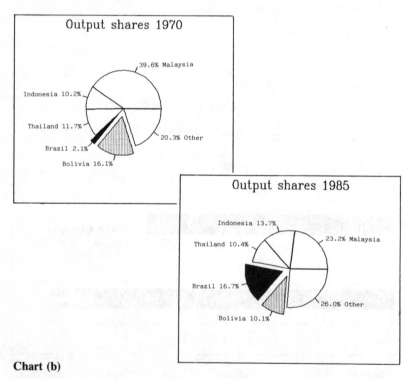

Chart (b)

This shows how Brazilian tin has forced its way onto the market, reducing the share of other suppliers, particularly Malaysia and Bolivia. It does not show the shrinkage in the overall market; losses are in fact more severe than indicated. Source: *International Tin Council*

The demand side

Tin has two major uses: in soldering in the electrical goods market, and in the manufacture of tinplate. Tinplate has fallen from 40.2 per cent of the total tin consumed in 1963 to 33.9 per cent in 1985, while solder has risen from 19.6 per cent in 1963 to 29.5 per cent in 1985.

A major use for tinplate is for cans. The box below looks in more detail at the history of the tin can. Differing amounts of tin can be used in tinplate manufacture. As explained in chapter 2, the demand for any commodity depends upon the technology of its use and upon

---

The rise and fall of the tin can

Tin, along with gold and copper, is one of the oldest metals known. It was first used in the early Bronze Age to harden copper and produce early human tools. The discovery of this process may have originated in the Iberian peninsula where there were easily accessible alluvial deposits of tin as well as nearby sources of copper. From there it spread to West and Central Europe, becoming a major commodity in the earliest forms of commerce.

Tin-bearing ores are associated with granitic rocks or the debris of such rocks. The only ore of economic significance is cassiterite which in its purest form contains over 78 per cent tin. The cassiterite occurs in thin, irregular veins or lodes, or in the debris which has built up from the gradual wearing down of tin-bearing rocks in alluvial deposits found in river beds and valleys, or on the ocean floor close inshore. The majority of tin production in the non-Communist world comes from these deposits. Southeast Asia is the main area of alluvial mining, while Bolivia has traditionally been the major source of tin from underground mines.

At the beginning of the seventeenth century a process of making tinplate was developed in what is today Germany by dipping iron plate into a vat of molten tin and draining off the surplus tin. The link between tinplate and the long-term preservation of food came towards the end of the eighteenth century. A Frenchman, Nicolas Appert, discovered that contact with air was the main cause of putrefaction in food and soon new techniques of food preservation were applied to containers made of tinplate. Tin was used as a thin protective layer on a base of mild steel; its properties of non-toxicity, resistance to corrosion and readiness to alloy made it ideal for the purpose.

John Hall and Bryan Donkin probably produced the first canned food in 1812. British manufacturers went on to dominate the industry. In 1856 they mechanised the hot-dipping of tinplate and improved the quality and lowered the cost of the steel base of

▶

the relative price of alternative materials. In the case of tin, demand fluctuates either because of the varying usage of tinplate or because less tin is used in each piece of tinplate. The latter occurs when tin prices are high relative to other metals. Tin use has come under pressure from other materials such as plastics and aluminium and from different methods of packaging and processing food (see box below). The rise in ownership of domestic refrigerators and freezers means that today people buy frozen peas whereas they once would have bought a can. Beer or soft drink cans, like the Coca Cola can, are now often made of thin aluminium.

tinplate. No major change occurred in the manufacturing process until the 1940s, when the hot-dipping process began to be replaced by the electrolytic deposition of tin on the steel base with a sharp reduction in the amount of tin used. But in the intervening years, the tin can — the major use for tinplate — had become a household word.

At the end of the nineteenth and beginning of the twentieth centuries canned food became increasingly important to the armies engaged in the various military campaigns from the Boer War onwards. By the end of the First World War, tin can production had become a major industry and the mass consumption of canned food amongst the population at large increased exponentially over the ensuing decades. Tinplate accounted for one-third of tin consumption by the late 1930s, rising to 45 per cent in the post-war years. But by 1984, it had declined to 34 per cent.

The past two decades have seen many changes in the can and packaging market. Substitution, technological change and, more recently, environmental concerns have all brought about a decline in tin inputs in this market.

There have been technological changes in the way the traditional tin can is produced, leading to ever thinner tin coatings on the tinplate. The ITC estimated in 1985 that tin used per unit weight of tinplate is falling at an annual rate of about 2.3 per cent. There has been growing competition in can-making and packaging from other materials. Tin has had to compete with aluminium and tin-free steels in the metal-packaging sector and with glass, paper and plastics in other areas of packaging. In recent years aluminium has consolidated its share of the beverage can market and increased its share of the food can market, though aluminium as well as tin is under threat from other materials, such as PVC beverage bottles and, in the food sector, new forms of plastic packaging.

There are many factors which influence choice of packaging material. They include raw material costs, energy used during

▶

42

manufacture, manufacturing costs, suitability for purpose such as corrosion resistance, consumer preferences and, increasingly, environmental and health factors. In the 1970s, for instance, campaigns were mounted in high tinplate consuming countries against non-returnable containers. Used alumunium cans are more economically recycled than used tinplate cans, and the aluminium producers have made a particular effort to establish the ecological advantages of their product. Social change in the industrialised countries has also affected tinplate consumption in a variety of ways. For instance, the growth of a market of single people living alone has led to experiments in single-portion, easily heated packages (possibly in a microwave oven) where plastics are more attractive.

The US has shown the most dramatic decline in tinplate consumption, although it is still the Western world's leading producer of tinplate. Tin-free steel now takes 25 per cent of the steel-based market in that country. The decline in tinplate consumption in Western Europe is less marked but the trend is clear. EEC tinplate consumption grew by only 1 per cent per annum in the 1970s compared to 4.5 per cent growth in the 1960s. There was a 2 per cent decline in the 1978-82 period, mostly from the UK, France and Italy.

Whether this trend will continue will partly depend on cost differences beween tinplate and aluminium. A recent comparison suggested that tin and steel are more likely to decline in price in real terms than aluminium, which could rise. This would increase the attractiveness of tinplate. Research has also finally come up with a an easy-open two-piece can end which will make it possible to recycle tinplate cans. This should enable tinplate to recapture some of the market share lost to aluminium. Tinplate is still preferred in the underdeveloped countries where the can has a low unit cost, long shelf life, strength and resistance to heat, humidity and corrosion. Mexico, Brazil and the Asian nations are building tinplate capacity in a move towards self-sufficiency and forcing production cutbacks in the EEC and the US. These are a few signs of hope in an otherwise gloomy future for tinplate.

A sharp fall in the costs of aluminium cans would lead to an increase in their use and a lowering of demand for tin. Alternatively, a big increase in aluminium prices might lead to more use of tin. The supply of aluminium in turn depends upon the technology of production and the costs faced by mining and processing firms in the aluminium industry. Aluminium, also a market in which oversupply has existed for some years, has been cheap enough to attract consumers. Some of the technical properties of aluminium and the fact that it can be recycled have increasingly led manufacturers to substitute it for tin.

Tin producers are, however, hopeful that the development of easy-open two-piece can ends will reverse the switch to aluminium, as it will then be possible to recycle tinplate cans efficiently. Such technological innovation, together with the fall in the tin price, may restore tinplate's competitive strength somewhat by the end 1987.

If tinplate has been an area of decline for the tin market, the boom in electrical goods has been a source of hope. It is unlikely, however, that

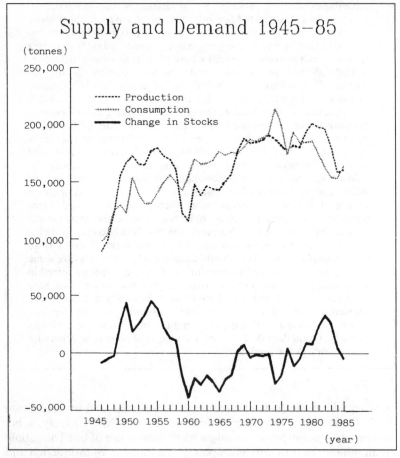

Chart (c)

The diagram shows that while tin stockpiles have been growing from 1980-85 (ie the thick black line is above zero), additions to stocks have in fact been decelerating and, since 1982, the problem of overproduction has eased. The collapse came when production and consumption were broadly in balance. Source: *International Tin Council.*

the demand for solder can grow fast enough to absorb the excess capacity of tin producers. In the period before 1974 there was a high correlation between the growth in consumption of tinplate and that of industrial output in OECD countries (the major industrial nations). This correlation has now disappeared so that even if more growth takes place in the advanced industrial economies, it gives no guarantee of an increase in demand for tin. The only other area which offers hope for tin consumption is in chemicals, a growing sector of tin consumption, but one which does not absorb very large quantities of the metal.

The disequilibrium of the tin market in recent times is illustrated by chart (c) which shows the imbalance between production and consumption between 1945 and 1985 and the additions to stocks. Some years of surplus are offset by years of shortage and the size of the stockpile itself has been relatively stable. Since the onset of world recession following the oil price rise, however, tin consumption fell sharply. In recent years it has been about 25 per cent below the peak year of 1973. Following the consumption peak (1973-77) the amount of tin produced was insufficient to meet demand and the excess had to be met from stockpiles. This demand, however, still continued to fall.

After 1977, production levels were consistently above consumption, perhaps responding too late to high consumption and thus high prices in the previous years. Production exceeded consumption for the six years 1978-83. The ITC had to increase the buffer stock and place controls on tin exports. In retrospect, it can be seen that this was not the first period of prolonged market imbalance; production was constantly in excess of consumption between 1948 and 1957, and there were shortfalls in each year from 1958 to 1966. But by 1983, as a result of the ITC's action, the situation had changed. Production and consumption were more or less in balance over the next two years.

Intervention and stockpiles

The history of the ITC is outlined in the box on page 46. It is important to stress that the ITC has been a successful example of commodity intervention, maintaining stability in a market which would otherwise have been subject to considerable volatility.

Nevertheless, it has run into a number of problems. Amongst them is the conflict of interests between rich consumer and poor producer nations. As the world economy entered a period of deep recession in the 1970s, this conflict sharpened. Major consumer nations elected right wing governments interested primarily in reducing inflation and cutting their domestic deficits. Indeed, low commodity prices have played a major part in their battle with inflation. These right-wing

45

The history of the International Tin Council

The International Tin Agreement was, until the crash, regarded as one of the most successful attempts at intervention in commodity markets. There is no need to suppose that, without the exchange rate shifts of 1985 (described on page 51), the agreement and the ITC which implemented it would have collapsed when they did. However, the history of the agreement does point to a number of recurring problems, of surpluses and shortages; conflicting interests between members and production by non-member countries. Nor can the role of the US be ignored. At the first international tin symposium held in December 1985, one of the presenters concluded: '...it can be appreciated that the United States has had a strong and largely disruptive influence over the world tin market for the last forty years.'

The first International Tin Agreement, which established the International Tin Council, was signed in 1931 by Malaya, Nigeria, the Netherlands East Indies and Bolivia, when overproduction and the great depression resulted in the collapse of tin prices. Production cutbacks did lead to increased prices and more producers were brought into the second and third agreements, the latter lasting until 1941. Excess production over quota by the major producers made the agreements shaky almost from the start.

Oversupply once more affected the market in the post-war period. At this time the US was building a stockpile of tin and foresaw shortages; it therefore opposed production cutbacks. But after the Korean War, the US stopped buying and prices slumped once more. Its stockpile would continue to play a major role in the story of tin. The US did not now oppose a new International Tin Agreement and took what has been described as an attitude of 'benevolent neutrality' towards the formation of the ITC in 1956 under the auspices of the UN, although did not itself join.

The ITC was to be a forum for both consumer and producer countries. Consumers were particularly concerned with the strategic importance of the metal, underlined when the Japanese overran the Southeast Asian tin fields in the Second World War and subsequently by the Korean and Vietnam Wars. The ITC was initially set up to deal with surplus production. It was authorised to set a floor and ceiling price for tin, impose export controls when necessary and establish a buffer stock.

By the mid-1960s, the dissatisfaction of the underdeveloped countries with existing trade patterns, the emergence of UNCTAD and the so-called North/South dialogue, provided the agreement with a new rationale. Emphasis was to be given to securing a price for tin in accordance with the development needs of the producers, not just the price which importing nations were prepared to pay. By the time of the fifth agreement in 1976, the UN had adopted a resolution calling for a new economic order and the agreement made explicit its objective to 'resolve problems relevant to tin by means of an international commodity agreement and taking into account the role which the International Tin Agreement can play in the establishment of the NIEO' (New International Economic Order).

But 1976 was also the year in which the US joined the agreement, deeply opposed in the wake of the OPEC oil shocks to producer cartels. It seems to have used its presence within the ITC to prevent action which might raise prices above market levels as a means of transferring resources to the producer countries. Some have observed that the US was more trouble within than outside the organisation.

Sales from the US stockpile had had a disruptive effect on the market since the end of the Korean War. By that time they amounted to 341,000 long tons of tin metal. In the 1960s, just as tin prices were recovering, sales from the US stockpile brought them down again, resulting in the reimposition of export controls in 1968. In the middle of 1973 over 42,000 tonnes were sold from the stockpile in an eighteen-month period and once again export controls were reimposed.

When it eventually joined the agreement, the US led the opposition of the consumer nations to raising the ceiling price and proposed that its stockpile sales be used to protect the ceiling and the buffer stock to protect the floor. In effect, this enabled the US to determine the highest level prices could reach. It insisted on a vote on every ITC decision, and as votes were distributed in proportion to a country's consumption or production and a two-thirds majority was required for a motion to be passed, the smaller nations found themselves with little influence. In this period the US succeeded in forcing through many of the rules which governed the Buffer Stock Manager's operations, so heavily criticised when the ITC collapsed in 1985. It refused to make voluntary contributions to the buffer stock and opposed moves to make consumers' contributions compulsory while pressing for a larger buffer stock to protect the floor.

The BSM complained publicly in 1979 about the failure of the consuming nations to make adequate contributions. His lack of purchasing power since 1977, he stated, had resulted in export controls to protect the floor, while the remaining buffer stock was not large enough to protect the ceiling.

The US did not recommence sales from its stockpile until 1981, although in the late 1970s demand for tin was at its peak and the buffer stock exhausted, sending prices beyond the ceiling and

▶

thereby encouraging production of more supplies. After production again exceeded consumption in 1980, the US Congress approved another round of sales from the stockpile at a time when prices were already in decline and export controls had to be imposed once again. This was the background to the attempt by a mystery buyer (since revealed to have been the Malaysian government) to control the market and push prices back up again. The failure of this attempt, followed by a continued fall in prices and the imposition of export controls by the ITC, eventually led to the formation of a producers' association — the Association of Tin Producing Countries (ATPC) — in 1983. It included Malaysia, Indonesia, Thailand, Australia, Nigeria, Zaire and Bolivia. The ATPC was something closer to the cartel arrangement the US feared so much, but as it emerged within the context of falling tin prices and world recession, its power could not be compared to that of OPEC.

Neither the US nor Bolivia joined the sixth ITA signed in 1982, in the midst of world recession. The US gave its reason as the failure to achieve agreement over a larger buffer stock, but the Reagan administration was deeply opposed to cartel-type organisations and suspicious of the ITA even though it included both consumers and producers. Bolivia, who had almost not joined the fifth agreement because the floor was lower than its mining costs, could not accept the export controls and buffer stock of the sixth. It did, however, join the ATPC.

A number of problems have beset the ITC in recent years, some arising from the inbuilt conflict of interests between consumer and producer nations, some from the changing world economic scene. These have been fully discussed in chapter 3. The immediate cause of the collapse of the ITC was a major unforeseen flaw in the agreement — the exposure to currency fluctuations — when the ITC decided in 1972 to set the floor price in Malaysian ringgits while financing the buffer stock in sterling. When cash and credit ran out for the ITC as a result of these currency fluctuations and the ITC member countries refused to come up with funds they had promised (the poor producers because they were unable to do so alone, and the rich consumers because they were unwilling to), the ITC was forced to default.

Whether, in view of all the pressures, the ITC had a long-term future is a matter for debate. Gill Burke, an academic who has studied the history of the ITC, suggests that if the members of the ITC had heeded the warnings of the Buffer Stock Manager and come up quickly with the funds to enable him to maintain the buffer stock, the ITC could have bought time. But, she writes: 'The fundamental problems of the ITC, of quota busting, of non-member producers and most of all of relationships between member nations, had all

▶

reached a point where a complete reappraisal was clearly necessary.'

The collapse of the ITC has been amply exploited by those who wish to leave everything to the market, but a new agreement might emerge in the future. The ATPC has tried to rally producers into making a new agreement. Its members have agreed to limit exports on condition that non-ATPC members, including Brazil, China and Canada, participate. Otherwise they would be making sacrifices from which those other countries would benefit. The ATPC has also promoted discussions under the auspices of UNCTAD to set up an international tin study group to collect and disseminate statistics and other market information. But differences between producers, some of whom can survive the present crisis, continue to beset the building of a strong producers' organisation.

What kind of agreement will eventually emerge is unclear, but many consumers as well as producers recognise that commodity agreements have an important role to play in bringing stability to markets; the producers would also like to see them contribute to a more equitable world economic order. In their 1985 annual review of the tin industry, Shearson Lehman Brothers, one of the key LME ring dealers in tin, referred to the idea of a free market for tin: 'We are somewhat schizophrenic over tin and do not take that view... we feel the tin market's best interests are served by an effective seventh tin agreement.'

governments have been opposed to UNCTAD's objective of using commodity agreements to redistribute income from the rich to the poor nations. The example of OPEC reinforced hostility to the very idea of commodity agreements.

The ITC has been criticised for holding prices at too high a level, but such criticisms take a short-term view of the market. If the price had been allowed to fall rather than production being cut back through export quotas, it would have resulted in short-term cheap tin and many mine closures. As supply fell, the price would in any case soon have risen again.

The comparison with OPEC is instructive. In 1973, OPEC, as a result of its market power, was able to increase the price of oil fourfold. This price bore no relation to production costs. In the case of tin, the production costs of those mines needed to meet demand (the marginal mines, ie the most expensive mines which could still stay in production) are not substantially below the price defended by the ITC. Massive supplies of really cheap tin are a myth. The ITC did choose to maintain prices by imposing export restrictions on its members rather than let the market impose production cutbacks through falling prices. In this way, the ITC avoided a more painful response to changing market conditions, paving the way for gradual adjustments. This could not be seen as a mechanism which transferred huge amounts of wealth to the tin-producing countries. The consumer nations represented on the ITC would have vigorously opposed its actions if that were the case.

It has also been suggested that by maintaining high prices, the ITC encouraged substitution away from tin. This argument is dealt with in chapter 2 (page 32). Substitution cannot be attributed simply to high tin prices. A whole range of factors have made aluminium and plastics more attractive alternatives to tin in packaging. Lower tin prices would not necessarily have halted the switch to other materials.

It was when Brazil began producing cheap tin, and demand for tin failed to expand, that problems inherent in the design of the ITC paved the way for its downfall. Whereas the ITC once controlled 75 per cent of world production, by 1985 it controlled only 60 per cent. The Buffer Stock Manager (BSM) was forced to buy greater and greater volumes of tin for the stockpile in order to maintain the floor price. By 1985, the stockpile exceeded 60,000 tonnes. The poor producer nations could not afford to finance this alone. The ITC member nations ignored the BSM's repeated requests for additional funds. Only the Association of Tin Producing Countries (ATPC), founded in 1983, offered £60 million, but this never appeared. The poorer producers were reluctant to give any of their scarce resources until the much wealthier consumer nations had shown their willingness to do so, and the richer producers were pursuing policies designed to depress prices rather than support them. In order to do his work, the BSM therefore had to borrow money using the tin stockpile as collateral, with disastrous results.

The collapse of the world tin market

By 1985 consumption of tin was low in relation to ten years earlier. But the fact that production and consumption of tin had in fact been broadly in balance over the previous two years suggests that adjustments were taking place amongst tin producers through the ITC's actions. The reason for the collapse of the tin market at such a moment has more to do with technical details of the operation of the tin agreement than with the underlying weakness of the tin market.

The BSM fulfilled his function of supporting low prices by buying tin when the market was weak. When further funds were not forthcoming

50

from the member nations of the ITA, the BSM had to fund tin purchases by borrowing from financial institutions. The tin stockpile was used as collateral.

In 1972, under strong pressure from Malaysia, the floor price of tin

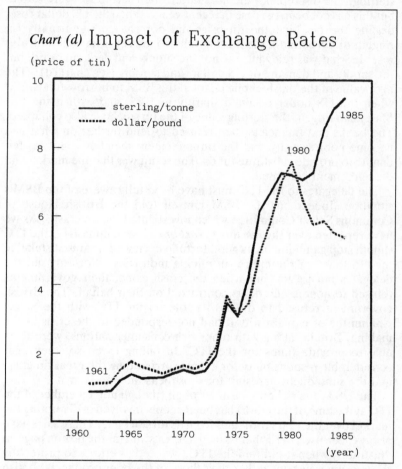

Chart (d) Impact of Exchange Rates
(price of tin)

Chart (d)

The sterling and dollar values of tin moved together until the arrival of the Thatcher government. The abandonment of exchange controls, the impact on sterling of high oil prices (with the UK in oil surplus) and the restrictive economic policies of the government all conspired to push the pound up. The resulting high value of sterling valued tin stocks allowed the Buffer Stock Manager to borrow in London. When the pound later collapsed so did the value of his collateral. Source: *Shearson Lehman.*

was set in Malaysian ringgits (tied to the US dollar). As Malaysia was the world's largest producer of tin it was considered more realistic to price the metal in their currency. But the funding of the ITC was not switched to Malaysian ringgits. The ITC's buffer stock was financed in sterling. The discrepancy did not matter when currencies were stable, but this has not been the case in recent years. When the US dollar rose, despite the fact that the tin price did not change significantly (in ringgits or US dollars), the sterling value of the ITC's tin collateral also rose; ie what was relevant was not the supply and demand of tin, but the supply and demand of US dollars and sterling (see chart (d)). The high value of the tin stockpile enabled the BSM to borrow funds. But when the US dollar declined sharply in 1985, and with it the tied Malaysian ringgit, the sterling value of the tin stockpile also collapsed. The banks and financiers then refused to lend further on what had become poor security and the tin agreement member countries felt unable to provide substitute funds. The result was that the market and the agreement collapsed.

The delegates to the ITC must have been fully aware of the BSM's situation. Indeed, as the BSM himself told the British House of Commons Select Committee which investigated the tin crash: 'As we have reported over the *last three years or so* [our emphasis] ...the ITC should stop gambling on its good fortune in view of what is at stake, ie the "fortune" of the entire tin mining industries.' Not only did the delegates fail to act, but when the crash came, their governments refused to honour the debts contracted on their behalf. The British government refused to discuss its role on the ITC with the Select Committee or explain why it had not responded to the crisis in the making. Britain, along with other rich consumer nations, were most able to provide funds for the ITC. In failing to do so, they bear considerable responsibility for events surrounding the great tin crash and the subsequent hardship for those least able to bear it.

The USA, the richest consumer of all (though not a member of the ITC at the time of the crash) has been deeply involved in disrupting the market over the years with sales from its tin stockpile. These sales have always been used to further its own interests and (as the box on page 46 illustrates) when it did join the ITC, devoted its efforts to protecting the consumer nations rather than those of the poor producers. It also bears responsibility for the problems facing the ITC by the early 1980s.

The *immediate* cause of the collapse of the tin market can be attributed to shifts in exchange rates. From this point of view, the collapse of the ITC can be seen as a sort of accident. The fact that the BSM was placed in a position so vulnerable to pressures of exchange rate adjustment points to bad design in the setting up of the scheme. But when the mechanism was devised, the sharp currency fluctuations seen in the past ten years, together with the total failure of the exchange rate stabilisation system set up at Bretton Woods at the end of the Second World War, could not have been foreseen.

The LME and the great tin crash

'The Metal Exchange as we know it ceased to exist on October 24.'

Michael Brown, LME chief executive

The tin crisis revealed serious flaws in the procedures of the LME. 'The customs and procedures of the London Metal Exchange have been tested to destruction', wrote the *Financial Times* in an editorial. 'The day of the traders' club where a gentleman's nod is his bond are probably over. The fact is that the potential danger in the tin market was visible for some time.' LME dealers had contined to sell tin on credit to the Buffer Stock Manager even though he was trading beyond his means. The ITC was building an ever bigger stockpile to maintain the tin price, buying forward quantities which it could not afford to take delivery of. The traders were making much money from the constant rolling over of these forward contracts without any adequate safeguards.

Relations between the LME and the tin producers were already fairly strained after incidents in which the LME was seen to intervene in the market with the effect of bringing the price down. The first was in 1982 when the Malaysian government attempted to keep the tin price up through a plan to corner the market. The Malaysian government argued that LME traders were depressing prices by selling tin they did not possess. It therefore began buying up forward tin from LME traders through a registered LME broker. As the moment approached for LME traders to deliver tin they had sold, they found they had none to deliver and many faced default. The LME immediately intervened to help them by reducing the penalty for defaulters. The tin price subsequently plummeted, leaving the Malaysian government with huge losses.

In June 1985 the LME intervened again in a way which convinced many producers that, far from being a free market, the LME was in fact clearly identified with the interests of the consumer nations. This time there was no attempt to corner the market. Tin prices had soared to £10,300 per tonne when LME traders found, once again, that they could not find the metal needed for delivery as contracts matured. There were accusations that they had been speculating on a collapse of the ITC and with it the tin price, by overselling and failing to cover themselves. If the tin price fell, those who had sold metal for future delivery would have made large profits. When traders were threatened with default, the LME suspended business ▶

53

and then changed the rules on default, reducing the penalties by nearly four times the previous figure. The tin price fell to £9,600 the day after the LME's action. Much of the tin that traders could not deliver had been bought by the ITC at the high prices and it lost a great deal of money through the LME action. All those traders who had covered their delivery commitments, including the ITC, were penalised by the rule change, while those who gambled against the ITC were let off the hook.

But LME traders certainly felt the impact of the crash when it came. When the Buffer Stock Manager defaulted, thirteen of the LME's trading companies and sixteen banks were left with the debts he could not repay and which the ITC member countries refused to honour. Customers who thought they had hedged against a fall in the tin price found themselves with tin stocks worth half the value they had been bought at. As a result, six of the twenty-eight companies trading on the LME have quit and confidence in it is severely shaken. Eleven LME brokers have set up a group called Tinco Realizations to try and pursue their claims in the courts against the member governments to honour the ITC's debts. But the ITC has claimed that, as an international body set up under the auspices of the UN, it is not subject to the law of any one country.

The events surrounding the great crash have reinforced those who for some time have argued that the LME should operate by a clearer set of rules. They have called for a clearing-house to record all deals (there has traditionally been no such record) and formalise a system of margin or deposit payments. At present, LME clients are not obliged to pay advance deposits and are given virtually unlimited credit. Such deposits would increase the costs of those who use the LME and perhaps reduce the level of speculative activity. A clearing-house would monitor operations and stand as a guarantor where a contract is threatened with default. It might not have prevented the tin crash but it would have sounded an early warning.

The LME told the British House of Commons Select Committee, which investigated the tin crash, that it was 'entirely blameless in this affair'. While they did not bring about the crash, LME traders were making profit from sales to the BSM on credit although they must have been aware of the dangers. In the words of a Tory MP on the Select Committee, they 'gambled and have now lost'. Confidence in the LME has suffered considerably, although many in the third world have felt that the LME has always reflected the interests of rich consumers and speculators. As one Malaysian commentator observed following the tin crash: 'The only conclusion we can draw is that the LME is a private club whose existence is only to serve its own interests'.

Whether the ITC would have survived, given the problems in the market, if the exchange rate shifts had not occurred is an interesting question. Its member producers would have had to face further cutbacks in production, but these could have continued to happen fairly gradually. The discussions within the ITC, which might provide some answers to the question, are still shrouded in mystery. The British government has steadfastly refused to comment on its role within the organisation. The evidence to the Select Committee suggests, at the very least, that insufficient ministerial attention was given to the body.

Ultimately the question may come down to one of political will. Many of the rich consumer nations of the ITC were fundamentally opposed to the idea of intervention in the market. As the box on the history of the ITC (page 46) illustrates, their reluctance to make adequate contributions is not a recent phenomenon; the BSM had complained publicly about this in the late 1970s. To the governments of these countries, the idea of providing sufficient funds to enable the ITC to ease the tin producers through the difficult process of adjusting to changing market conditions was simply not on the agenda. Although they had benefited for many years from a stable tin market, they allowed the crisis to develop rather than give the ITC adequate funds to carry out its work, refusing when the crash came even to honour the debts for which many deem them responsible. After all, they will not bear the brunt of large-scale mine closures and job losses on the scale of Bolivia or Thailand.

Shaking out the weakest

Before the tin market collapsed, it had been adjusting, if slowly and painfully, to the situation of oversupply. The end of the system of intervention in the tin market has had two consequences for people who work in the tin industry. First, the stabilising effect of an intervention system has gone, and there is an acceleration of the process of adjustment. Second, the liquidation of the ITC stockpile now means that a huge volume of tin has become available to the market. It is equivalent by itself to about six months of normal world production. With such an amount of tin dominating the market, prices are set to remain low for some time. Malaysia has cut production in the year since the crash by about 25 per cent, while Bolivian output is estimated to have fallen from about 16,000 tonnes in 1985 to about 11,000 in 1986.

The speed with which the crisis has bitten does not, however, mean an end to low prices. Although output of existing mines has fallen

55

steeply and mines are closing, prices could remain very low for as long as it takes to soak up the excess material contained in the former stockpile. By the end of 1986, estimated output was about 130,000 tonnes, down from 159,000 in 1985, running about 25,000 tonnes per year below consumption. Stocks of tin which stood at 110,000 tonnes at the time of the crash, were down to 80,000 tonnes a year later. Most of the ITC's 16 banking creditors subsequently sold their stocks, but the biggest four creditors with the largest stocks are still awaiting the outcome of suits against the ITC as well as a further rise in the tin price. They have between them 40-50,000 tonnes. Current stocks still represent about six months' non-communist world tin consumption. The USA has 120,000 tonnes in stockpile, which it is selling at some 3,000 tonnes per year. The most optimistic forecasts suggest a price of £6,000 per tonne by the end of 1987, but there are still many uncertainties.

The issue for Bolivia is whether, even after so much pain, it will still have a place as a producer of tin for world consumption. There is now competition in the true sense of the word. The market is operating without safeguards; there are no government agreements and there is a serious imbalance between supply and demand. Large-scale mine closures are guaranteed, but each one which occurs increases the chances of survival of the others. The key question is: Which producers will give way? For Bolivia, the odds are worsened by the performance of its mining industry in the recent past, as the next chapter will explain.

4 Bolivia and tin

'If it is true that Bolivia is a country so rich in raw materials, why is it a country with so many poor people. And why is its standard of living so low in comparison with other countries, even in Latin America?'

With this question, Domitila de Chungara, a Bolivian miners' leader and the wife of a miners' leader, puts her finger on a paradox which has struck many who have visited Bolivia or studied its economic development. The fall in world tin prices has highlighted the problems of the Bolivian economy still further, exacerbating a situation the roots of which go back a long way.

From the Spanish conquest onwards, Bolivia (or Upper Peru, as it was mostly known until independence from Spain) was integrated into the world economy through its mines. Until the end of the last century, Bolivia's role was that of silver producer for world markets. At the beginning of this century, tin replaced silver as the key export.

The growth of the armaments industry in Europe and North America, plus the invention of the tin vacuum-packed can, produced a surge in the demand for tin. Output in Bolivia expanded faster than in other producer countries. Bolivia accounted for 11 per cent of world production in 1900; by 1921 this had climbed to 26 per cent. In 1945, after several years in which Malayan tin supplies to the West had been cut off by the Japanese invasion, Bolivia's contribution reached the exceptional, all-time high of 48 per cent of world supply.

Until 1952, control of Bolivia's tin mining business was in the hands of a group of local capitalists known collectively as the 'tin barons', or the *rosca*. The wealthiest and most powerful of these was the Patino family. Simon Patino is a classic case of 'rags to riches'. By a stroke of good fortune he gained a concession at Llallagua in the north of Potosi department; it became known as Siglo XX-Catavi and turned Patino into one of the world's multimillionaires. Among his other interests, Patino's empire vertically dominated the tin business in mining, processing, transport, banking and smelting. In 1924, he acquired the world's major tin foundry, Williams Harvey near Liverpool in England. Patino's main rivals — far behind him in the production league — were the Aramayo and Hochschild groups. Aramayo's group controlled a cluster of mines close to the town of Potosi and two

57

important mines, Caracoles and Viloco further north, close to La Paz. Hochschilds owned La Unificada in Potosi as well as the San Jose and Colquiri mines in Oruro.

Tin mining in the first half of this century was a highly lucrative business. In many cases, tin ores were to be found in the same geological formation as silver, so old silver mines and the infrastructure connected with them were used by the tin mining companies. Initially, at least, ore grades were high and the mineral deposits reasonably accessible. Average tin content of the rock mined was nearly 7 per cent in the 1920s, compared with 0.98 per cent in 1970. Wage costs were minimal, investment costs slight, and the 'tin barons' successfuly exercised their political influence over successive governments to keep taxes down.

In this way, Bolivia became involved in world trade virtually as a monoexporter with all the vulnerability that this implied. In 1950, for example, mining accounted for 95 per cent of Bolivia's exports and tin for 74 per cent. Although as a share of profit tax payment was small, for central government tin export taxes paid by the mining companies were the major item of income. In common with other mining economies, tin extraction did little to develop the Bolivian economy. However, in comparison with other producer countries with much larger populations such as Malaysia, Indonesia and Thailand, Bolivian miners formed a larger proportion of the working population. But even at the peak of its production, mining as a whole never accounted for more than 5 per cent of the labour force, while its contribution to Gross Domestic Product (GDP) seldom rose above 10 per cent. The majority of Bolivia's population is involved in agriculture, still the largest single item of GDP. Almost all inputs connected with the mining industry — clothing, basic mechanical items and even some food such as wheat flour — are imported. Low wages in the mining industry mean that mining activity does little to stimulate other economic activity by way of consumer demand. Furthermore, the development of the country's infrastructure has been tailored to the needs of the mining companies. Railways were constructed linking the mines with the Pacific ports, but it was not until 1953 that Bolivia's main towns — La Paz, Cochabamba and Santa Cruz — were linked by road.

In 1952 a revolution took place in Bolivia whose impact at the time was comparable to that of the Mexican revolution of 1911-17. The well organised and combative tin miners were able to force the new government (headed, in fact by Victor Paz Estenssoro, the President who took office again in August 1985) to nationalise the property of the *rosca* and create a new state mining corporation, Comibol.

Subsequent governments have tried to reduce the country's

58

Statue of the miner, Potosi

Julio Etchart

Siglo XX miners demonstrate in La Paz for a minimum living wage

Julio Etchart

dependence on tin exports by promoting other export sectors; notably cash crop agriculture, crude oil and natural gas. As a consequence, tin's contribution to total exports declined as other sectors grew. The contribution of the mining sector as a whole to total exports of goods fell from 90 per cent in 1970 to 62 per cent in 1980, and the share of tin dropped from 45 to 40 per cent of exports. Similarly, as new sources of tax revenue came into being, the contribution of mining — most of it derived from tin — fell from just over two thirds in 1970 to around one-quarter in 1980.

However, as we shall see, this relative decline in Bolivia's dependency on tin reflects not just the growth of other sectors, but an underlying decline in tin mining itself. Even so, the tin industry — and the metallurgical industry which is closely tied to it — continues to have an economic importance for the Bolivian economy which far exceeds that of any other major world producer of tin. In 1984, tin still accounted for 34 per cent of exports, compared with 3 per cent in Malaysia, 1.25 per cent in Indonesia and 3.1 per cent in Thailand. It is therefore an economy which is far more exposed not only to normal price variations but to artificial price shocks from, for example, the sale of the US strategic stockpile, which has been used at various times to influence domestic politics. The workings of central government and decentralised agencies are still highly dependent on income from tin royalties. Their diminution in recent years has contributed greatly to the perennial public sector deficit, as have Comibol's operational losses. Finally, mining and metallurgy in Bolivia have until recently provided a livelihood for some 76,500 families: 27,000 in Comibol, 7,200 in the privately owned *mineria mediana* (medium sized mines), 16,700 in the smaller-scale mines and some 25,000 in small mining cooperatives. The great majority of these are involved to some extent in tin mining.

The miners in Bolivia

In the town square of most Bolivian mining towns is a statue of a miner, drill in one hand and rifle in the other. The statue is a symbol of and tribute to the militant tradition of the Bolivian miners. Among the most disciplined, organised and class-conscious of all workers in Latin America, the Bolivian miners have tenaciously fought for better conditions of work — safety, pay, housing and food — sometimes by violent means. Inevitably they have clashed with the other most disciplined and organised grouping in Bolivian society — the military. The clash between miners and the army is a persistent theme in Bolivian politics. Indeed, it is no accident that there are military barracks close to all the major mining centres in Bolivia. The geographical isolation of the Bolivian mines, the appalling living and working conditions in them, and the traditional degree of human solidarity which exists in most mining communities anywhere, have provided the context for strong trade unions. But it has been the pivotal role of tin mining in the Bolivian economy which has given the miners' union, the Trade Union Federation of Bolivian Mineworkers (FSTMB), such strong political leverage. Strikes in the mines prior to nationalisation led to a succession of clashes between miners and troops. In Siglo XX, Patino even contributed to the troops' pay. The miners' organisation took a major step forward, however, with the formation of the FSTMB in 1944.

Slow, silent death

The cemetery creaks. Beneath the graves countless tunnels have been dug, with openings barely wide enough for the men who disappear into them, like rabbits, in search of tin. New deposits of tin have accumulated through the years in the tons upon tons of slag piled up in huge gray mounds across the landscape. When the violent rains pour from low clouds over Llallagua — where men drink themselves into a desperate stupor in the *chicha* taverns — one sees the unemployed crouching beside the dirt roads to collect the tin as it is washed down. Here, tin is an omnipresent canned god reigning over men and things. There is not only tin in the bowels of Patino's old mountain; the black sparkle of cassiterite betrays its presence even in the adobe walls of the camps. There is tin, too, in the yellowish mud that slides off the slag, and in the poisoned water that flows from the mountains; it is in earth and rock, surface and subsoil, in the sands and pebbles of the Seco riverbed. In these dry and stony regions almost thirteen thousand feet above sea level, where no grass grows and everything — even the people — is the dark color of tin, men stoically endure their enforced separation from the joys of the world. The camps are a huddle of one-room dirt-floor shacks; the wind howls through cracks in the walls, cutting to the bone. A university study of the Colquiri mine found that of every ten boys questioned, six sleep in the same bed with their sisters...

We were deep down inside the Juan del Valle mountain. Hours earlier the siren shrilly summoning workers of the first shift had resounded through the camp. Going from gallery to gallery inside the mine, we had passed from tropical heat to polar cold and back again to the heat, always — for hours — in the same poisoned air: humid, gas filled, dusty, smoky. Breathing it we could understand why miners lose their senses of smell and taste in a few years. They all chew coca-leaf and ash as they work, and this too is part of the

▶

annihilation process, for coca, by deadening hunger and masking fatigue, turns off the alarm system which helps the organism stay alive. But the worst of it was the dust: circles of light from the miners' helmets danced dimly in the gloom, showing thick white curtains of deadly silica. It does not take long to do its work. The first symptoms are felt within a year, and in ten years one enters the cemetery. Late-model Swedish drills are used in the mine, but the ventilation system and work conditions have not improved with time. Up on the surface, independent workers use twelve-pound wooden sledgehammers to conquer the rock, just as they did a century ago, as well as antique pumping devices and sifters to collect the mineral. They work like dogs and are paid in pennies, but they have the advantage of fresh air over the underground workers, prisoners sentenced without appeal to death by asphyxiation.

The din of the drills stopped and the workers took a break as we waited for more than twenty charges of dynamite to explode. Death in the mine can also be quick and thunderous: it is enough to miscount the number of detonations or to leave a wick burning longer than it should. Or a loose rock, a tojo, may crash on your head. Another form of death is by bullet: St John's Night 1967 was the latest bead in a long rosary of massacres. At dawn soldiers took up kneeling positions on the hillsides and fired volley after volley into mining camps lit by bonfires for the fiesta. But slow, silent death is the mine's speciality. Vomiting blood, coughing, the sensation of a leaden weight on the back and acute chest pains are the signs that herald it. After the medical diagnosis, pilgrimages to an endless chain of bureaucrats. You are allowed three months before eviction from your house.

E. Galeano, *Open Veins of Latin America*

British miners visit Bolivia

Safety regulations practically do not exist. The miners are not supplied with adequate clothing and in some cases are not supplied with masks. In all cases the masks are inadequate as they were developed for mining at sea level. The filters are so heavy that they cannot breathe properly at 12,000 ft. The miner therefore tends to replace the mask with a handkerchief which gives little or no protection against the dust. Only when blasting does he use the mask, removing it immediately afterwards and returning to work.

Silicosis is rampant among the Bolivian miners. Though no statistics are available, it is estimated that an underground worker contracts first degree silicosis within five years. At the age of 30, he ►

The miners played an important role in the course of the 1952 revolution, in which the army was partially dismantled and, in some of the mining areas, replaced by popular militias. They assumed a special status in the newly formed Bolivian Workers Congress (COB) and won a certain degree of worker participation (*cogestion*) in Comibol following nationalisation. Though linked to the ruling Nationalist Revolutionary Movement (MNR), the miners showed a keen sense of independence in resisting a US-inspired stabilisation plan in 1956, and subsequently a joint plan to restructure Comibol, known as the *Plan Triangular*, financed by the US and West German governments and the Inter-American Development Bank. Both these initiatives sought to achieve lower manning levels and a reduction in miners' effective wages by eliminating subsidised food in the mining communities. International institutions such as the World Bank have long attributed many of Comibol's problems to the political muscle of the FSTMB.

Interview with a miner's wife

'We all have large families, six or seven children. There are no opportunities for advanced education in the mining areas. They have to go away, and we have to pay for their food, their clothes, their lodging. They get very demoralised. They ask, why should I stay at school, I'm never going to get to the university.

'You've seen the company store. It's packed full with food, isn't it? There's everything there. The miners have everything. That's what they say to the tourists. It's full because we haven't got the money to buy anything. Recently a lot of TV sets, fridges, electrical goods, record players, have gone on sale, things we don't need. We don't have meat, what do we want with fridges? They make us want them and we get in debt. Every worker owes 20,000 to 30,000 pesos. When he gets paid he owes half already. Before he buys food he has to pay for the TV set, the fridge. Then the miner dies and his wife ▶

64

doesn't get a pension. It goes to pay off the debt. She doesn't even have a house.

'There's always been a lot of discrimination against women. We were never allowed to try and solve our own problems. But we were forced to by the situation here. In 1961, the women started to organise here to get their husbands out of prison. They had been put there by the goverment. We went on hunger strike and we got them out. Women have to participate, it's wrong to expect men to do everything. We used to shout and fight with our husbands because the children didn't have shoes, because they didn't have enough to eat. But then we realised that our husbands are killing themselves in the mine, that they don't get paid for the sacrifice they make. It's not them we should be shouting at. We organised the housewives' committee in 1961. Then they started to persecute us as well. I was in prison three times. I lost a baby. I was eight months pregnant and they beat me so badly that I lost it.

'Bolivia is a rich country. But it needs capital to exploit its resources. It comes from outside, especially from the United States. They direct the repression too. We are working to pay our oppressors.

'At the moment our organisation exists, but it's clandestine. It was banned by the government. We are affiliated to the Miners' Federation and the Bolivian TUC. We participated in all the strikes. Now there's not much we can do. It's getting worse.

'My husband works down in the pit extracting the tin. He earns 28 pesos a day. He could earn more blasting but we want him to live longer. We have eight children alive, the eldest is eighteen and the youngest ten months. Each one has a job to do. We make *empanados* [meat pasties] and sell them outside the company store to get money. There are always long queues outside the company store, you sometimes have to queue for half a day. We get up at 4 o'clock to make the *empanados* and work till 11.00. If we sell them all we get an extra 30 pesos. If there are any left I give them to the children. Not everyone is as lucky as I am. Everyone knows me, so they buy my *empanados*. There is a lot of competition to get selling them.

'We are desperate now. But we can't do anything. Please try and do something to help us. We are honest workers. We have only asked for the right to organise, the right to a decent life. They say that foreigners pay us to make trouble. How can we be in contact with foreigners when the Bolivians themselves don't know what's going on?

'Our men die young, they die just when our children need the guidance of a father, when they need more food and attention. There are hundreds of widows wandering around here with nowhere to go and with nothing to feed their children. There's no work for ▶

young people. When the father dies the eldest son has to take charge of the family. Then he gets married and has his own children and has to take care of two families. They all live together. We live in a small room and a kitchen. There's no space for the children to play. You've seen how they throw our houses all together, and with all the mines there are they don't even give our children a space to play.

'We get films here. They bring them from the United States. They are degenerate films and they don't care who sees them. Our children can go and no one stops them. It's part of their policy to pull us down even further. Why don't they bring educational films? Why don't they bring films that will teach our children something?

'Women have to suffer a lot here. We bear a lot of children. When she is pregnant she doesn't get enough to eat. She has to work and carry around heavy packs on her back. She has to stand in the queues outside the general store. This causes a lot of miscarriages. The men drink a lot. It's the brutal work in the mine and the atmosphere here that does it. Then they beat their wives and they lose their babies. The atmosphere in our *campamentos* is bad. When the wind blows the dust rises from the mudpits. The women and children suffer a lot from lung problems.

'We have to be mothers, wives, cooks, cleaners, workers and pack animals, 50 per cent of our children die. I would like my son to study, but he will probably replace his father in the mine.

'Here we are tied to centuries of tradition. My husband gets teased if I don't send his food to the mine on time. They ask him, „What is she doing? Probably off in that union. You should beat her, then she would keep in line.„ It is difficult for a woman to participate. When we started they called us prostitutes. I know a man who was exiled to Argentina. They kept telling his son that he was exiled because his mother was involved in politics.

'Once they doubled the price of tinned sardines. We got together and went to La Paz to protest. They told us there was a scarcity, the prices had to go up, there was nothing they could do about it. We didn't know then that they have a reserve for times of scarcity to keep prices the same. We have to study, read and talk to people. They are against education, it's too dangerous for them.

'They call us terrorists. But they are the only terrorists. It's not the people who massacre and kill. During the last strike they came looking for me. They knew I was eight months pregnant and even went to the hospital and searched it bed by bed. I was hiding in the mine, three days in the mine, sometimes in total darkness. I had to come out, I was almost suffocated by the gas. I ended up in hospital for two months. They wouldn't let anyone see me. I was expecting twins and one of them died, killed by the gas when I was in the mine. They owe me two babies now...'

Report of National Union of Mineworkers Delegation, 1977

For nearly twenty years from 1964 to 1982, Bolivian political life was dominated by a succession of military governments, most of which sought to quell the trade unions, in particular the miners' union. They tried to build alliances with more conservative groups of workers, attempting to set up parallel unions. They militarised the mining centres and exiled union leaders. But though they managed to silence the unions temporarily, they never succeeded in destroying them. Even the peculiarly vicious regime of General Luis Garcia Meza (1980-82) which vowed to destroy the union once and for all — symbolically pulling down the FSTMB's offices in La Paz — was unable to prevent protracted and overtly political strikes in the mines.

Massacre

The military coup in 1980 heralded a major offensive against the miners. What follows is an extract from an account given by some of the women of the mining community of Caracoles who survived an army massacre in August of that year:

'The Max Toledo Regiment from Viacha, a sector of the Tarapaca Regiment and the Camacho Regiment from Oruro attacked Caracoles with guns, mortars, tanks and war planes; our husbands defended themselves with stones, sticks and dynamite. By Monday afternoon most of the miners were dead, and the survivors either fled to the hills or houses in Villa Carmen. Army troops pursued them and killed some men in their homes, arrested and tortured others and bayonetted many. They also decapitated the wounded.

'In the middle of the plaza they put dynamite in the mouth of one miner and blew him to pieces... They whipped children with cables and made them eat gunpowder. They made young people lie down on broken glass and forced us to walk over them; afterwards the soldiers marched over them... they did not hesitate to rape us and also adolescent and little girls. At dawn on Tuesday... they loaded the dead and wounded into three army trucks headed for La Paz.

'By Friday they were still bringing prisoners bound with wire. The women were forbidden to pick up the dead and give them a Christian burial on the pretext, „There is no order.„ Then on Friday they gave us an order to go for the dead, but we only found jackets, trousers, sweaters, caps, shoes and other things soaked with blood; the bodies had disappeared. Some were thrown into a grave behind the cemetery; we were not allowed to identify them. About 900 people disappeared, the dead, wounded and prisoners.'

LAB, *Bolivia Coup d'Etat*

Since 1982, the miners and the COB have vehemently opposed the implementation of another IMF-backed stabilisation plan. A series of economic 'packages' involving massive devaluation of the Bolivian peso, huge food and petrol price hikes and cuts in subsidies and other government spending, have led to strikes not only in the mines, but also by most other sectors of the workforce.

The strength and resistance of the Bolivian miners clearly reflects their strategic place among the country's labour force. Any strike in Comibol has an immediate impact on the inflow of foreign exchange and on government revenues. It is the knowledge of their economic weight which has so often encouraged the FSTMB to fight on despite apparently insuperable odds. The miners' endurance also clearly owes much to the social cohesion of the mining communities and their radical tradition. Miners' leaders have proved very difficult to intimidate or co-opt.

But it is perhaps their degree of unity which most distinguishes the Bolivian miners from other Latin American workers. Attempts to set up parallel unions have all been stillborn despite often generous official patronage. Unity, however, does not mean a lack of internal political conflict. The factionalism which divides the Bolivian left is omnipresent in the unions. But in the FSTMB, like the COB, trade union unity has tended to prevail over inter-party strife.

This unity owes much to the strength of trade unions and the weakness of political parties in Bolivia. The country's political parties evolved late in the day. The Communist Party, for example, was established as late as 1950. Whereas unions have long had an organised presence in most sectors of the workforce, political parties often function as little more than personal platforms for individual political leaders and lack mass support or organisational structure.

Because of their militant tradition, tight organisation and bargaining strength, the miners have always occupied a special place within the COB. They have traditionally held the top union posts — with miners' leader Juan Lechin Oquendo occupying the post of Executive Secretary from its birth in 1952 until 1986 — and have had a major say in the formulation of COB policy. However, in recent years, this dominance has been reduced as other groups of workers have begun to play a more forthright role within the COB, in particular, the factory workers and organised peasantry. Furthermore, the strength of the miners has been considerably sapped by the country's recent economic crisis.

The making of the tin crisis

The Bolivian tin crisis has been a long time in the making. It dates not from the suspension of trading in the LME in 1985, nor from the slide in tin prices which began in 1980. Nor did it begin, as many argue, with nationalisation in 1952. It dates from the 1920s and 1930s.

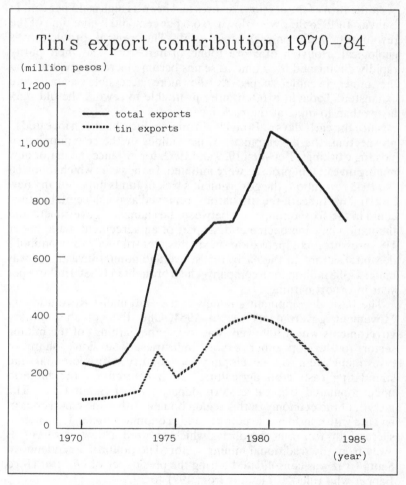

The declining importance of tin for Bolivia's exports can be seen from this diagram. In the early 1970s, tin provided half the country's exports. By the 1980s, this was closer to one-quarter. Although the available statistics are not up to date, figures for more recent years would show an even more distastrous fall. Source: Banco central de Bolivia, ITC.

As early as 1936 a British Board of Trade report noted the speed at which Bolivian ore grades were falling, and with them the profitability of Bolivian mining operations. The author of the report argued strongly that if money were not invested in the discovery of new tin deposits, Bolivia would soon run out of the mineral on which its economy had become so dependent.

At the turn of the century, tin ores had been as high as 15 per cent in Bolivia. In 1926 they were down to 6.6 per cent and by the time of the revolution, were only 0.9 per cent. The central problem was geological. Bolivian ores are found in hard rock and their purity rapidly diminished over time as seams became increasingly thin, and the mines became deeper as the more accessible seams were exhausted. Today it is often more profitable to rework the old slag-heaps than to mine at the rock face.

Since the early days of Bolivian tin mining, little has been invested in prospecting, the development of new mines or the re-equipping of existing workings. Between 1929 and 1952, for instance, no major new mining investment projects were initiated. In the years which followed the 1952 revolution, the government's lack of funds impeded any new investment. Indeed, the 'tin barons' removed as much capital as they could in the six-month period between the change of government and the nationalisation decree and, as part of an agreement made under US pressure, compensation payments contributed to Comibol's decapitalisation. In the early 1950s, average annual investment was under US$5 million for a company which brought in US$60 million per year in export earnings.

The basic development strategy of the Nationalist Revolutionary Movement governments up to 1964, and that of the military governments which followed, was to use the earnings of the mining sector to develop other export industries. The lion's share of investment went on developing the country's oil potential and stimulating cash crop agriculture. Both centred on the hitherto underpopulated tropical eastern department of Santa Cruz. The growth of the economy in this region bought with it the emergence of an elite with considerable political and economic muscle. They used it successfully to promote policies which ensured a flow of resources away from the traditional mining sector. The political ascendency of Santa Cruz was consolidated during the presidency of General Hugo Banzer who ruled as dictator from 1971 to 1978.

The main thrust of successive governments' policy towards the mines was the attempt to increase productivity by reducing manning levels and lowering miners' pay. The clearest example of this was the *Plan Triangular*. Though the results of this were not as dramatic as Comibol's more vehement critics would have wished, miners' wages fell in real terms during the 1950s and 1960s, while the number of jobs dropped from an all-time high of 36,000 in 1955 to around 22,000 in 1970.

Under the Banzer regime the mining sector benefited little from the borrowing bonanza which quadrupled the foreign debt between 1971 and 1976. As before, credit went to build up agriculture and the oil industry. Within the mining sector, however, the growing private sector did relatively better than Comibol. Some twenty-five companies make up the so-called *mineria mediana*, and of these the biggest were all linked to international mining interests. The average value of fixed assets in the *mineria mediana* doubled between 1974 and 1976; and while the *mineria mediana* increased its share of total mining exports, it enjoyed more favourable tax treatment than Comibol.

State investment, however, did go into building up Bolivia's metallurgical capacity. Following the establishment of a national smelting body (ENAF) in 1966, a tin smelter was set up at Vinto in 1971 and was expanded in 1977. The basic idea was to cut dependence on smelters in the US and Britain, enabling Bolivia to increase its range of markets and contribute value-added to mineral exports. But while debt servicing outpaced the generation of extra export earnings, new plant failed to take falling mineral output sufficiently into account, with the result that ENAF has suffered badly from underused capacity. Financial headaches were increased by a variety of technical problems which have dogged the development of smelting plants.

However, irrespective of these problems, high prices for minerals on world markets during the 1970s created a climate of optimism. The world price of tin, for example, rose from US$1.69 per fine pound* in 1971 to US$7.61 in 1980. Mineral exports rose accordingly. Tin brought in US$102 million in 1970, and by 1980 exports of tin were worth US$378 million (see chart, page 69).

Deterioration

Though high world prices encouraged increased production, Bolivia's total output of tin concentrate — that of the private mines and cooperatives in addition to Comibol — actually fell from 29,397 tonnes in 1970 to 26,771 in 1980. Labour disputes played a part in disrupting production, especially between 1978 and 1980, when several attempted military coups provoked a series of strikes. But the main problem was the fall in ore grades. Greater efforts had to be made to recover ever diminishing quantities of tin and, as a result, labour productivity declined. By 1980 the average ore grade for Comibol's mines was as

*Bolivia calculates the tin price in terms of pounds of contained 'fine' tin to the US dollar. (2,204.72 'fine' lbs = 1 metric tonne).

71

low as 0.58 per cent. Whatever the reasons, however, it is quite clear that the high prices paid during the 1970s for Bolivia's mineral exports were disguising deep-rooted problems of falling production.

These difficulties were further exacerbated by the debt crisis. Under President Banzer, debt accumulated rapidly because borrowing was cheap and Bolivia's repayment capacity seemed fairly sound due to growing oil exports and high mineral prices. Indeed, the Banzer government, anxious to go down in history as the great 'moderniser', displayed a seemingly insatiable appetite for credit. By the beginning of the 1980s, however, developments undermined the country's credit-worthiness. Surpluses of crude oil for export had dried up, the value of mineral exports began to drop sharply and the interest payable on the debt rose as dollar interest rates went up and dollar inflation went down.

Bolivia fell further and further into arrears on its debt repayments from 1982 onwards. As lending to Latin America as a whole dried up in the wake of the Mexican debt scare, new loans were no longer available to Bolivia and vital trade credit was reduced to a trickle. In turn, the acute lack of foreign exchange helped push Bolivia towards a twin spiral of massive peso devaluation and hyper-inflation, feeding off each other. By 1985 Bolivian inflation, at 8,163.4 per cent per year, was the highest in the world. The peso, which had been 25 to the US dollar in 1980, rocketed to 9,000 at the end of that year and to over one million by September 1985.

The effects of the debt crisis hit the mining sector very badly. First, imports were slashed as dollars became unavailable; total imports were halved from US$828 million in 1981 to US$412 million in 1984. During this period it became almost impossible for Comibol to acquire vital pieces of machinery and spare parts. The most common reason for breakdowns in production was the failure of machinery which, most observers agree, was in any case better suited to a mining museum than to practical use in the industry.

Bolivia's high-cost mines

Most veins worked today are narrow (no wider than 10 centimetres in the case of tin), and mining entails the removal of an unusually large proportion of worthless host rock to extract the payable ore. Drilling (the most costly element in hard rock mining) is slow, wear on bits heavy and consumption of (imported) explosives high; once mined the broken material is relatively more expensive to mill than is softer rock. Typically the veins vary substantially in thickness and tenor and many peter out over short distances. Most are steeply

▶

---

inclined and the ores they contain often change their character with depth: near the surface they tend to be oxidised, richer, and easier both to work and concentrate, whereas at depths below, say, 100 metres, the harder, leaner sulphide ores are the norm. The veins are frequently fractured and faults dislocate the geological structures in which they are contained. It is not easy to predict the possible extension of metaliferous structures and the problem of proving reserves and extrapolating likely levels of future mineral production are more taxing than in many other competing mineral fields. Individual deposits are small and the potential for economies of scale limited. Mines that are large by Bolivian standards are only modest by world standards...

The value of most Bolivian deposits is further reduced by their scattered distribution, inaccessibility and inhospitable setting... In the vicinity of Lake Titicaca and La Paz the granites form the seemingly indestructible core of the highest sierras of the glacial Andes; further south recent layers of volcanic outpourings blanket part of the mineralised zone, obscure underlying geological relationships, and make veins difficult to locate. It is thus no accident that the most important mining region of Bolivia coincides with the widest and highest part of the Andes thereby creating mining conditions of almost unparalleled difficulty.

No other country has to contend with mining at such altitudes as does Bolivia. All but 10 per cent of her production is from mines above the 3,700 metre contour line or over 12,000 feet above sea level... The mountainous situation of most mines hampers their access and increases their costs...

The high costs individual mines have to bear because of their isolated and mountainous local situations are compounded by the remote and land-locked situation of the country at large. Metals or concentrates leaving Bolivia, like mining supplies entering the country, have to bear the cost, say, of a 1,000 kilometre journey overland by truck or rail, perhaps even by lake steamer, between the mine and Antofagasta, Arica, Mollendo or Matarani on the Pacific coast. These ports were lost to Bolivia and gained by Chile or Peru a century ago following the War of the Pacific: at best their foreign ownership is a source of constant irritation to the Bolivians, at worst a potential stranglehold on the economic lifelines of the country. Once at the Pacific coast there is a 10,000 kilometre journey by sea to the major world markets for Bolivia's minerals. In 1915 such transport costs represented one-quarter of the total cost of placing Catavi tin on the market; fifty years later the figure was still a considerable six per cent with half the cost being incurred by the journey from the mines to the Pacific.

The methods of mining used in Bolivia reflect the predominance of small and dispersed deposits and of vein ore rather than ▶

disseminated ore, the disadvantages of geographical location, and a shortage of investment capital. For example, it has so far proved impossible to use modern methods of bulk mining in Bolivia. Rather, the typical mining practice in Bolivia is that of selective underground mining using methods that were commonplace at the beginning of this century and a technology which is largely of nineteenth-century design. This means both that the costs of mining per unit of production are, in general, higher than those of competitors, and also that the costs of mining form a higher proportion of total realisation costs than in most other mining fields. The driller and his gang remain the key figures in most Bolivian mines and each block of material dislodged underground is handled by several pairs of hands before it reaches the mill. The whole operation is relatively labour intensive. For example, Catavi has as many personnel on its payroll as does Chuquicamata, the great open pit copper mine in Chile where over 30 times as much material as at Catavi is extracted each year. On the positive side it can be claimed that mining generates a larger number of jobs than would be the case if more capital intensive methods were used. Bolivia has no shortage of potential miners and needs employment opportunities for them: the cost of labour is governed by the local labour market and paid for in local currency, unlike almost all the capital equipment and material needs of Bolivia's mines. On the negative side, however, Bolivia is swimming against the modern tide, and in consequence has been unable to keep abreast of some of the more recent innovations in mining and drilling... Old-fashioned working techniques and outmoded and worn-out equipment help increase unit costs, squeeze profits, reduce the opportunity for re-investment, and lessen the likelihood of external financing. The geological and geographical difficulties of proving reserves, of planning their exploitation and of winning a return on them makes Bolivia a technically higher-risk country for new mining ventures than most others. Mining expertise may be able to counter such risks but it is a very mobile factor and there is a strict limit on the availability on such talent, even in a mining country like Bolivia.

David Fox, *Mines and Mining in the Americas*

Second, with the official exchange rate of the peso always lagging behind its value on the parallel market, Comibol was severely penalised by having to convert its foreign earnings into pesos at a highly overvalued rate, resulting in grotesque distortions in its accounts, massive losses and progressive decapitalisation. Third, investment in the state sector — including prospection — was less than US$5 million per year in the 1980-84 period. Unable even to pay miners' wages, it is not perhaps surprising that the limited amount Comibol assigned to investment was sucked into current spending. Finally, the succession of economic 'packages' decreed first by the military governments between 1980 and 1982, and then by the constitutional Siles Zuazo government of 1982-85, led to a series of general strikes and several lengthy stoppages in the mines.

Output figures for Bolivian tin and other minerals show the seriousness of the problem, even before the catastrophic fall in tin prices at the end of 1985. Whereas in 1981 national output of tin concentrates was 27,612 tonnes, by 1985 it was down to 16,136 (see chart, page 76). Comibol's production fell slightly faster than the national average; from 18,586 tonnes in 1981 to 10,038 in 1985. Given the fall in the world tin price from an average US$6.42 per fine pound in 1981 to US$5.60 when the LME stopped trading in October 1985, the value of Bolivian tin exports fell even more rapidly than production in those four years; from US$343 to US$187 million. And since in Bolivia most key minerals — tin, lead, silver and zinc — are mined together, falling tin output has been mirrored by falling output for other export minerals. As a whole, the mining sector brought in US$592 million in foreign exchange in 1979 (70 per cent of total exports) while by 1985 it was worth only US$264 million (45 per cent of exports).

The deterioration of the mining economy and the exchange rate distortions meant that the losses incurred by both Comibol and the smaller private mines began to pile up. According to official estimates, Comibol's losses for the five-year period 1980-85 were as follows (in US$ millions):

1980	1981	1982	1983	1984	1985
30.0	45.4	51.9	51.6	68.5	165

By 1985 they were a massive US$165 million, equivalent to the export earnings from tin concentrates and metals for the whole country.

The disastrous performance of the mining industry served to underline the extent of the crisis in the country as a whole. In the export sector the only bright spot was the increasing income from natural gas sales to Argentina, which by 1985 was by far Bolivia's most important single source of legal foreign exchange. Unfortunately, Argentina was the only customer in the absence of pipelines to alternative markets. A relatively small amount of foreign exchange comes back into the domestic economy from Bolivia's other main export, cocaine.

The kiss of death

When the LME suspended trading in tin in October 1985, the world price stood at US$5.60 per fine pound. In the wake of this, Bolivian tin

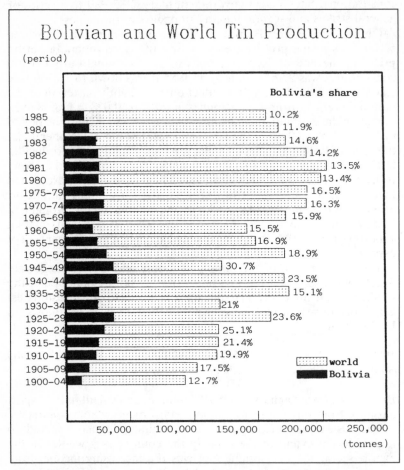

Bolivian and World Tin Production

(period)

Bolivia's share

Period	%
1985	10.2%
1984	11.9%
1983	14.6%
1982	14.2%
1981	13.5%
1980	13.4%
1975–79	16.5%
1970–74	16.3%
1965–69	15.9%
1960–64	15.5%
1955–59	16.9%
1950–54	18.9%
1945–49	30.7%
1940–44	23.5%
1935–39	15.1%
1930–34	21%
1925–29	23.6%
1920–24	25.1%
1915–19	21.4%
1910–14	19.9%
1905–09	17.5%
1900–04	12.7%

world
Bolivia

50,000   100,000   150,000   200,000   250,000
(tonnes)

These percentages demonstrate how the world is no longer reliant on Bolivian tin. Between the wars Bolivia produced up to one-quarter of the world's supply, while in the immediate post-war period it met over 30 per cent of the world's tin needs. By 1985 it supplied only one-tenth of a market which has shrunk sharply since 1981. Source: *International Tin Council.*

was being traded at as low as US$2 per fine pound.

Bolivian tin is amongst the most expensive to produce in the world, with an average cost of production of US$6.47 per fine pound. Even at a world price of US$5.6 per fine pound, most Bolivian mines, including all those in the public sector (with the important exception of Huanuni) operate at a loss.

The drop in the world price will further exacerbate Comibol's losses which have been building up since 1980. One official estimate for 1986 losses, based on the supposition of an average tin price for the year of US$3.50 per fine pound and made in January of that year, put the losses at US$182 million. According to other analysts it could be a great deal higher, depending on whether or not attempts to cut losses are implemented. The FSTMB, however, was slightly sceptical about the size of estimated losses and accused the government of exaggerating the scale of the problem. Official estimates indicate that Siglo XX-Catavi would be the biggest single loss-making mine, accounting for US$32 million alone. Next would be Colquiri, with losses of around US$14.9 million. Comibol's volatilisation plant at La Palca near Potosi seemed set to lose US$37.1 million. In fact, this plant was out of action during the first four months of the year owing to its high production and energy costs.

The panorama was no less gloomy at ENAF which, again according to the official estimates, was set to lose US$40 million in 1986. Apart from the financial crisis prompted by low tin prices, ENAF also urgently required a big cash injection simply to prevent the plant from grinding to a halt because of the lack of maintenance and repair work in recent years.

The 1985 tin crisis took place as a new government came to power led by the veteran politician, Victor Paz Estenssoro. Supported by Banzer's extreme-right Democratic Nationalist Action party (ADN), Paz's right-wing MNR opted to go for shock treatment in a bid to achieve hitherto elusive support from the IMF for debt rescheduling.

New Economic Policy

One of the cornerstones of the so-called New Economic Policy was to be radical changes in the way Comibol was run. This was part of a total package of economic measures which included a massive devaluation of the Bolivian peso from 75,000 pesos per US dollar to 1.1 million pesos, a freeze on wages and an end to government subsidies on food and fuel. In addition, the New Economic Policy proposed to 'decentralise' certain state companies including Comibol, while liquidating others such as the Bolivian Development Corporation (CBF). Decentralisation was widely seen as the first step in a strategy of selective closures and the privatisation of remaining mines.

The New Economic Policy

Right wing plans for reactivating the Bolivian economy came to the same conclusion: the deficit was the result of excess demand (even though Bolivia is the poorest country in Latin America after Haiti). To wipe out the deficit, therefore, consumption had to be restricted by freezing wages and increasing prices... by abolishing protectionism and returning to economic liberalism.

General Banzer had promised 'surgery without anaesthetics' if elected, but it was Paz Estenssoro, thought initially to be more moderate, who applied the iron fist. On August 29 the flotation of the peso (with a hidden devaluation of 1,300 per cent) was announced; wages and salaries in the public sector were frozen and prices were freed; restrictions on 'hiring and firing' were abolished; and the denationalisation and privatisation of the main state enterprises, Comibol and the Compania Nacional de Petroleo were put on the agenda...

Which economic groups stand to benefit from these policies? Sectors dependent on exports, particularly mining, stimulated by a more 'realistic' exchange rate and the return to a free market in minerals; financial groups; and finally those involved in commerce, including contraband and drug trafficking. Representatives from these groups are also the brains behind the austerity policies: Guillermo Bedregal, who became Foreign Secretary in the Cabinet reshuffle of 22 January 1986, is adviser to a subsidiary of Markrich, a transnational specialising in the gold market... Juan Careaga, Minister of Finance, is an influential banker, and Carlos Morales is president of the Confederation of Private Industry.

How will such measures affect the gulf between rich and poor?... Salaries were not frozen for all social classes: members of parliament and the military hierarchy were able to increase theirs substantially.

For those whose wages were frozen, the problem is how to make ends meet with rises in the cost of living of between 100 and 150 per cent...

In the short term, every national industry is condemned to death, beginning with agricultural produce, [especially] sugar... poultry... meat... and even rice... The number of workers sacked in the capital recently was estimated at 10,000 in the private sector. In the public sector 30,000 have already been made redundant...

What will happen to these people? The best possible alternatives are colonising the lowlands, contraband and cocaine trafficking. Nonetheless, the New Economic Policy (NPE) seems to satisfy the IMF which is paying the first instalment of $50 million to Bolivia, a third of its standby credit.

At the same time, Washington, which had supported Banzer, is also happy: the policies of Paz Estenssoro are attractive to foreign capital and the Bolivian government signed an agreement with the Overseas Private Investment Corporation (OPIC), the north American institution which protects private investments abroad. Bolivia is also one of 15 countries with priority access to the Baker Plan.

Le Monde Diplomatique, March 1986

Officially, government strategy was to 'rehabilitate' Comibol, although the proposals themselves contained nothing new. The main features of 'rehabilitation' were a freeze on wages, closures and an end to the system of subsidised food supply. These, as we have seen, had surfaced earlier in the *Plan Triangular* during the early 1960s. In April 1981, during the Garcia Meza dictatorship, a rehabilitation plan had also been launched, backed this time by the World Bank. However, it was jettisoned when the popularly-elected Siles Zuazo government came to office. Instead, workers' participation in Comibol's management was introduced following pressure from the FSTMB and the COB, with the FSTMB controlling a majority of seats on the board. But Siles' defeat and the electoral humiliation of the left in the 1985 elections meant that the World Bank's plans were quickly resuscitated. Bolivia hoped to get up to US$200 million from the World Bank and other institutions to initiate a serious investment programme in mining.

The collapse of the tin price speeded up the pace of the government's proposed changes. A cabinet reshuffle in January 1986 underlined the hard line approach, a sine qua non for IMF assistance. Gonzalo Sanchez de Losada, the major shareholder in Bolivia's leading private mining company, Comsur, took over the key Planning Ministry. The threatened drop in tin exports to US$100 million in 1986, coupled with the obvious impact that this would have on government revenue, made a deal with the IMF much more urgent for the government. As if to coax Bolivia along, the IMF offered US$57 million to compensate for the fall in tin prices.

For Comibol, rehabilitation came to mean the closure or at best 'cooperativisation' of many of the country's mines. A recommendation submitted to President Paz in January 1986 stipulated the following: the permanent shutdown of the Siglo XX mine; the temporary closure of the Mina Matilde and the dismissal of all staff except the maintenance workers; the closure or

79

'cooperativisation' of Corocoro and Colquechaca; the closure of Comibol's metallurgical plant in Oruro and the temporary closure (pending conversion to gas fuel) of the Palca volatilisation plant. It also specified a reduction in manning levels through early retirements and voluntary redundancies at Quechisla, Huanuni, San Jose, Caracoles and Viloco. The memorandum also mentioned the possibility of turning La Unificada in Potosi into a cooperative, with new cooperatives being recognised legally. This scheme, if implemented, would totally transform the state mining sector and deal a mortal blow to the FSTMB, whose strength historically has depended upon negotiating with a single employer.

By the middle of 1986, workers were already beginning to leave the mines as *relocalizacion* became the catchword in government circles. Retirement notices had been issued to over 5,000 workers in early 1986 although, as many soon found out, Comibol did not have the money to pay the promised severance payments to the miners on retirement. Government proposals had been drawn up to relocate miners in gold-panning projects in the jungle regions of La Paz and Pando departments, and in colonisation projects in Cochabamba and Santa Cruz. The latter would involve opening up uninhabited jungle land to agriculture.

None of these projects was given any detailed thought by the authorities and no provisions were made with respect to housing or health care. As a result, they have never got off the ground. Most of the miners who did leave seem to have headed to the coca-producing area of Chapare where good money was to be found preparing cocaine paste. Ironically, at the same time, the US government was trying to get Bolivia to clamp down on coca growers and processors.

Mobilisation of the workers

The response of the miners to the New Economic Policy was strike action. The mines were shut down throughout September 1985 and in many of them miners organised a mass hunger strike underground in protest. Of all groups of workers, the miners were the most directly affected by the New Economic Policy. It froze their wages, ended the system of subsidised food sold at company shops, eliminated the FSTMB's majority *cogestion* and threatened the entire structure of Comibol which had ensured the FSTMB's influence in the past. The mobilisation of workers to oppose the New Economic Policy was orchestrated as in the past by the COB. Other groups of workers supported the disciplined lead set by the miners. But by the third week, support for the miners' cause was wavering, and even in the mines it became increasingly difficult to sustain the strike. As the strike continued, it became obvious that, given the low price of tin on the world market, strike action suited Comibol's management very well because it freed them from their contractual responsibility to pay wages.

In the meantime the miners and the FSTMB continued to reiterate their whole-hearted opposition to any plan of temporary or permanent closure of mines, and urged the government to design a policy which avoided redundancies. The most forthright stance was that taken by the Siglo XX-Catavi workers. With the local union led by a former Trotskyist, Filemon Escobar, the Siglo XX-Catavi miners urged their fellow workers to do everything within their power to stop the closure of mines. They put forward a document known as the 'Catavi thesis'. They argued that their own experience showed that by operating the mine themselves, they could increase production substantially and reduce unit costs through working other parts of the mine or eliminating bureaucratic waste. The priority for them was to preserve jobs and thus maintain the unity of the mining communities:

> The revolutionary role of the proletariat at this time is defined in one single objective: the unyielding defence of national production, beginning with the defence of Comibol. We must not allow any enterprise to close. One effective form of struggle is to maintain our productive apparatus fully operational. The productive apparatus must not be paralysed. When that happens, demoralisation sets in and the working class falls apart.
>
> The strength of the working class lies in the survival of the productive apparatus. Until recently, the political and union struggles of the exploited were possible because Bolivia had an important productive base. Today, this is almost impossible. And our struggles at the political level were much more effective and significant because we miners were the heart of the national economy. The republic depended upon us for its livelihood. This was why the victory of April 1952 was possible. We shouldn't forget that the Catavi Mine alone produced 1,200 tons a month, exporting more than 15,000 tons of tin a year. That was the power of the miners and in particular the power of the miners of Siglo XX and Catavi.

Other FSTMB members, however, were critical of this approach, and argued instead that the rehabilitation of Comibol depended on the nationalisation of the *mineria mediana*. They pointed out that private companies such as Emusa, Comsur and International Mining had been much more successful than Comibol in diversifying out of tin into other minerals such as antimony, zinc and gold. These views were put forward by a group of radical-left parties called the 'Eje de Convergencia Patriotica' (literally the Axis of Patriotic Convergence), which at that time controlled the COB.

The debate around these two positions predominated in the 21st Congress of the FSTMB, held in Oruro in May 1986. The 'Catavi thesis', which seemed to reflect more closely the immediate preoccupations of the rank-and-file, was finally adopted by the Congress. FSTMB leaders, Juan Lechin and Victor Lopez, who had supported the losing position, resigned as a result. They were succeeded by Simon Reyes, Filemon Escobar and Justo Perez.

Matters were given new poignancy in early June, when the government precipitately ordered the closure of the Mina Matilde, a mine producing mainly zinc on the northeastern shore of Lake Titicaca. Miners' leaders at Matilde roundly blamed the loss of up to 600 jobs on Comibol's failure to invest in the mine or at least provide vital spare parts to keep machinery going, or tap extensive known silver and lead deposits in the same region. In July, the FSTMB published its own set of emergency proposals to deal with the crisis along with a plan for the rehabilitation of Comibol (see page 87). The FSTMB was determined that the era of tin was not yet over.

5 Bolivia: the end of the tin era?

Bolivia's economic prospects over the next few years seem bleak. Production levels in 1986 fell again for the sixth year running, legal export earnings are at their lowest level since the mid-1970s, and national income per capita will reach its lowest point in over thirty years.

In the mining sector there is little evidence to suggest a strong and sustained increase in prices for any of the minerals which Bolivia currently produces and exports. This sombre picture for mining is paralleled for different reasons in Bolivia's other main commodity exports. Unless substantial new reserves of crude oil are discovered, Bolivia will continue as a net oil importer. Natural gas exports, which in 1983-85 compensated for Bolivia's poor mineral export performance by providing over half its foreign exchange earnings, are threatened by the development of gas fields in southern Argentina. Argentina is in a good position to dictate the terms at which it buys Bolivian gas; in May 1986 it revised the price paid downwards from US$4.27 to US$3.70 per thousand cubic feet. This meant a reduction of estimated gas revenues from US$373 million in 1985 to US$330 million in 1986. In the agricultural sector, exports of sugar and cotton show scant likelihood of ever being able to generate much more than a small fraction of exports.

In contrast with Bolivia's legal or 'formal' economy, the 'informal' economy has been booming in recent years. Only the existence of this huge sector, involving activities unregulated by any legal constraints, explains how Bolivians have weathered the present crisis.

The most important 'illegal' export is, of course, cocaine. Bolivia and Peru together corner the world market as producers of coca leaves, the basic raw material for cocaine. Production of coca has soared since the 1970s in response to almost insatiable demand for cocaine in the US, and Bolivia's exports of cocaine paste have jumped accordingly. No one knows with any accuracy what cocaine is worth to Bolivia. One estimate puts coca production at 160,000 tonnes in 1985, sufficient to produce 437 tonnes of cocaine with a street value of US$3.3 billion in Miami. Most Bolivian producers receive nothing close to the US street prices and the bulk of the foreign exchange they earn ends up in 'safe' Caribbean or Swiss bank accounts, not in Bolivia. Moreover, much of the wealth which enters Bolivia takes the form of contraband produce — digital watches, whisky, transistor radios — rather than dollars. Those dollars which do come in tend to be spent on high living or real estate, and do not find their way into productive investment — still less into the Treasury or the vaults of the Central Bank.

While drug money does little to benefit Bolivia's development, coca and cocaine have become a major source of employment generating a livelihood for as many as one in every six Bolivian families by 1985. With the recession hitting mining, oil and manufacturing, increasing numbers of Bolivians found themselves migrating to coca-producing areas such as Chapare in the north of Cochabamba.

Panning for gold along the rivers flowing northward and eastward towards the Amazon was another popular option. Communities sprang up in previously deserted jungle areas in the north of the La Paz department and in Pando on the country's northern frontier with Brazil. Gold retrieved in this way was sold not to the Banco Minero in Bolivia, as it should be, but in Argentina and Brazil, where prices were higher and payment was in harder cash than the Bolivian peso. Another source of economic activity was the import and export of contraband across unguarded land frontiers.

Alternatives

It was against the background, therefore, of a burgeoning 'informal sector' that the collapse in tin prices occurred. It brought seriously into question Bolivia's future as a tin-based economy and brought into sharp relief the consequences of the loss of employment in the mines. *Relocalizacion* of mine workers meant in effect leaving the mining communities for work as a *contrabandista*, gold panner or cocaine producer.

Opinions differ on the prospects for Bolivia's untapped mineral reserves. According to one leading mine owner in the private sector, exploration had only been undertaken over 5 per cent of the total area where mineral reserves are currently found. The extent of known but untapped deposits of other minerals reinforces the view that Bolivia could break its dependence on tin. Gold, for instance, is to be found not only in the rivers of the northern jungle, but at La Joya in Oruro, Rio San Juan del Oro in Potosi and in Los Lipez in the extreme south of Potosi.

Another form of diversification would be to exploit the lithium and potassium deposits of Coipasa and Uyuni. Bolivia has the world's largest known deposits of lithium which, if extracted and sold, could bring in as much as US$350 million per year in foreign exchange. At the same time, Bolivian mining engineers are convinced that new deposits of zinc, silver and lead could be exploited, and that tin smelters at Vinto could be adapted to process other metals. Unfortunately, there is no indication of a consensus being reached over how these mineral resources should be tapped.

Future prospects

The question facing Bolivia is whether tin has a role in the country's economic future. Many on both sides of the Bolivian mining industry — management and workers — believe the tin crisis need not be the end of the line for Bolivian tin mining; and that once short-term difficulties have been overcome, Bolivia could continue to play an important world role as a producer of ores and metals. This confidence is based partly on the conviction that world mineral prices will eventually pick up again, even though the specific problems affecting tin might suggest that recovery in the tin industry will be slow.

There are disagreements as to what is needed to save the industry and how much can be saved. In the private sector, mine owners are anxious to see the frontiers of the state rolled back once and for all, with the privatisation of Comibol's potentially more lucrative operations. On a general level this is a view which has struck a chord inside the Paz Estenssoro administration, with which the business community has links. It is also a view which finds favour at the World Bank and the IMF. In discussions with the IMF to arrange a US$50 million standby loan during the first half of 1986, the government made it very clear that the 'restructuring' of Comibol was a key factor in its overall strategy to reduce the country's chronic deficit. In addition, it seems highly probable that World Bank assistance to the mining sector was conditional on restructuring. At the same time, the government made clear its interest in increasing the volume of foreign capital in mining, through either joint ventures or direct investment.

Such ideas, however, were and are anathema to the FSTMB, the COB and the left-wing political parties. For them, any restructuring of Comibol should mean a reaffirmation of state control, guaranteeing worker participation in management, the channelling of necessary funds to recapitalise the industry, and the non-payment of Comibol's foreign debt obligations.

85

The miners' campaign

The FSTMB argues forcefully not only that the government has deliberately exaggerated the size of Comibol's losses in order to justify mine closures, but also that effective steps could be taken to reduce this year's shortfall significantly. This could be achieved, they say, by exempting Comibol from paying taxes and royalties, by reducing the charges made by the state companies for electrical energy and rail freight, and by ending the system whereby Comibol, rather than the Ministries of Health and Education, pay for medical services and schools in the mining communities. Redundancies could be avoided if Comibol were better administered, and if it made the sustained effort necessary to diversify out of tin by exploiting Bolivia's potential as a

---

The Quixote spirit

Filemon Escobar is a miners' leader from Catavi with many years of participation in union and political affairs. The following is part of an interview he gave about the tin crisis in Bolivia:

'The important thing I want to say is this: The Bolivian working class has never been interested solely in obtaining better working conditions and higher wages. It is a social class which sees its role as transforming the country through its productive capacity. This is its great merit.

'If you go to the mining camps of Siglo XX, which date from the time of Patino, you will see that we don't have running water nor bathrooms. I am telling you this to show you that we have never won social improvements like the proletariat in the west. In Siglo XX nobody changes his shirt every day, and we don't have consumerist values. Our diet is simple. Our meals are a soup with pasta followed by rice, or a soup with rice followed by pasta, sometimes mixed with a little bit of potatoes.

'It seems to me that this class, which has never won for itself the right to a decent house, nor even a reasonable wage, that doesn't have access to any social security system and that doesn't say I have to earn so many dollars an hour like the labour movement in the west, has instead a greater task to fulfil.

'Just as we live with conditions which date from the time of Quixote, we need the spirit of Quixote now, to tranform the nation. Our march on the first of May should reaffirm our will to save Bolivia from becoming a country living on drugs, smuggling and speculation in the black market. We have to become a country dedicated to production, even if this doesn't mean great improvements in our living standards. The important thing is to save our sense of being a nation.'

producer of a wide range of other minerals. Closure of mines now, argues the FSTMB, would make it excessively expensive to reopen mines when prices rose once again.

The FSTMB's case was put forward in July 1986, in a plan which aimed to address both the emergency situation and the long-term rehabilitation of Comibol (*Plan de Emergencia y Rehabilitacion de Comibol*). The plan set out in detail how costs could be cut and output increased, and rejected the closure of any mine without a prior technical and economic survey. Such a survey should also take into account the likely recovery of mineral prices and consumption by 1990, by which date the rehabilitation plan for Comibol could be in full operation.

In August, the miners began their campaign against the government's plans for Comibol. The government was due to announce the decree which would restructure Comibol that month. An indefinite hunger strike was launched on 13 August, and a 'march for life and peace' was organised. There were signs of a considerable reactivation of the popular movement in Bolivia, with miners receiving wide support from peasant, worker and student organisations. A national campaign, not just against the Comibol proposals but also against the government's economic strategy as a whole, was seen by many as the only way to save the mines.

The march (from Oruro to La Paz) began on 22 August, the day the government announced the main points of its plan. Full details of the plan were published in Decree 21377 on 26 August, followed a day later — when the march had reached Calamarca — by the declaration of a state of siege. The government's plan was presented in terms of 'decentralising' Comibol into independent administrative units. There would be two divisions: the Department of Mining Companies and the Department of Metallurgical Companies. Only the profitable mines would be kept working. A few others would be maintained for purposes of exploration for new reserves and some, the weakest and least profitable, would be 'cooperativised'. These included the Catavi, Siglo XX, Colquiri, Colquechaca, Chorolque, Japo, Morococala, Machacamarca, Santa Fe and Viloco mines. In this way, the miners themselves would take responsibility for the unprofitable mines. They would have to pay an annual rent for them but no capital would be provided by the government. The government's aim was to pave the way for handing over the most profitable mines to the private sector. In the meantime this plan would force more miners out of the mines, destroying the power of the FSTMB.

Miners' leaders at first rejected the decree, which they claimed would 'end the nationalisation of the mines and the gains of the 1952 revolution'. FSTMB leader, Filemon Escobar, told miners that the

Federation was proposing that Comibol be handed over to the workers to be administered by the FSTMB, making use of the money which the government had set aside for its restructuring programme. But on 29 August, with the marchers surrounded by troops, the FSTMB leaders changed their position and sought dialogue with the government through the mediation of the church.

There was considerable debate amongst the miners on the course to follow; the housewives' committee favoured continuing the march to La Paz, others favoured staying in Calamarca and continuing the hunger strike while negotiations went on. However, the leaders opted for an organised retreat with a commitment to dialogue. Miners' families continued the hunger strike in their mining towns, still winning support from many sectors of the popular movement, but without official support from the leadership of the FSTMB.

Union leaders argued that their action was necessary to avoid a wave of heavy repression which would have hit not only the miners but the popular movement as a whole. They also maintained that grass-roots support was still weak as many miners were seeking higher redundany payments rather than backing a broader strategy of opposition to the government. But others argued that the leaders had seriously weakened their bargaining power in negotiations by not maintaining the march and the maximum organised strength the popular movement could muster.

Leadership crisis

The miners are the backbone of the COB; their return home meant the end of any coordinated national struggle against the government. Many miners were confused and frustrated by the decisions of the leadership and clearly sensed their weakness. There were proposals from a number of mines that if Comibol was not to be turned over to the FSTMB, then the maximum amount of redundancy payments should be negotiated.

The FSTMB reached an agreement with the government which was announced on 13 September. It left the main features of Decree 21377 intact. The miners' leaders agreed to put an end to pressure on the government, including the hunger strikes which were still continuing. In exchange, union leaders imprisoned under the state of siege were released. Implementation of the proposals for cooperativisation was suspended while studies were carried out on their viablility.

The government acknowledged under the agreement that its aim was not to dismantle Comibol but to rehabilitate it. But mining minister, Jaime Villalobos, made clear in a statement on 16 September that the 'agreement signed with the Miners' Federation doesn't alter anything substantially, because the cooperativisation programme is still going ahead, decentralisation and the decision to eliminate Comibol's deficit will continue'. Just days after the agreement was reached, on 16 September, the US government approved a short-term bridging loan of US$100 million and the Bolivian government immediately signed a 'letter of intent' with the IMF and were granted a further US$75 million to ease the balance of payments crisis.

The agreement was subsequently rejected by the rank-and-file of the FSTMB, which had not been consulted before it was made, and the executive committee was forced to resign. An extraordinary Congress of the FSTMB was called in October to resolve the leadership crisis.

The Catavi thesis, which had been approved at the May Congress, had come up against a number of problems. The thesis placed a priority on defending jobs, but many miners felt they could no longer survive in the mining areas, given the conditions there (outlined in chapter 1), and they opted to leave. Many were aware that in leaving the mines they were weakening the FSTMB and the COB, and that there was no guarantee that redundancy payments would be paid or that they could find work elsewhere. But many preferred to take the risk. The government's intransigence and virtual abandonment of the state mining sector also made it very difficult for miners to continue working in order to prove the viability of the mines as the Catavi thesis proposed. By August strike action had begun and it was evident that the Catavi thesis could no longer be sustained.

Although political divisions produced intense debate at the extraordinary Congress of the FSTMB in October, in the end the Congress was notable for the degree of unity which was achieved. A major issue was whether to fight for higher redundancy payments for miners who opted to leave the mines, given that the government itself was trying to encourage voluntary retirement. The Bolivian Communist Party rejected such action on principle, whereas the Catavi and Siglo XX miners had accepted it as a major demand along with the defence of Comibol and wage increases for those who were prepared to stay in the mines. Even before the Congress they had decided to organise a march on La Paz in support of these demands. But the final documents, approved by a large majority, centred on the points which united the movement: the defence of the state mining sector on the basis of the FSTMB's plan, and the fight to meet people's basic needs, including wage increases. Victor Lopez and Simon Reyes were once again elected to leadership positions in the union.

By the end of 1986, Comibol was still intact as the proposals for decentralisation had not as yet been formally implemented. But the state mining corporation was clearly a shadow of its former self.

Production estimates for Comibol in 1986 were only 4-6,000 tonnes, compared with a target of 13,680 tonnes. The virtual abandonment of the nationalised mining industry signalled its death. The FSTMB remained resolutely opposed to the government's proposals. But they were forced to concentrate their efforts on negotiating compensation for redundant miners.

International forces versus popular movement

The miners have a very uncertain future before them. The Bolivian government remains firm and confident in its plans for the industry, and is backed by powerful international forces. It looks to external funding as the only way out of the present crisis. 'Bolivia has no other solution than international credit', finance minister Juan Cariaga declared in September 1986. Its neo-liberal economic programme appeals to the major lending institutions, the IMF and the US government. It is a programme which minimises the role of the state and looks to the private sector to reactivate the economy. The restructuring and rationalisation of state enterprises such as Comibol is an integral part of the government's strategy. However, while the government's 'shock' programme has reduced inflation, it has not resulted in any reactivation of the economy. The private sector is not investing and the Bolivian economy remains in a critical state.

The Bolivian government has no serious policy for the country's economic future. It is merely responding to short-term pressures. The miners, on the other hand, are prepared to make sacrifices for long-term gains for Bolivia as a whole. The FSTMB emergency plan for the mines is a reasonable one for the future. The immediate problem is survival while the effects of the tin crash continue to be felt. This requires international as well as national action; for instance the re-creation of the stockpile would help Bolivia weather the present crisis.

While Bolivia can no longer be a major tin producer, the era of tin need not be over once and for all. Reducing costs could enable some production to continue. Bolivia has few alternatives other than cocaine to its immediate problems of employment and foreign exchange shortages. Maintaining some of the country's tin industry on the basis of the miners' plan would at least ensure a livelihood, if a meagre one, for some of the population and allow time to search for new areas of productive activity. This would undoubtedly require considerable economic assistance from national and international sources. More importantly, it would need political will. But the government of Paz Estenssoro is eager to seize an opportunity to do away once and for all with a thorn in the flesh of Bolivia's armed forces and government: the country's tin miners.

The government is undoubtedly stronger and the miners weaker than in the past. The collapse of Bolivia's nationalised tin industry has severely affected the FSTMB and Bolivia's labour movement as a whole. The social and political identity of Bolivia is undergoing considerable change, whose outcome is still unclear. Much now depends on the reactivation of the popular movement: not just against the government's plans for the mines, but against the New Economic Policy and all it implies for the people of Bolivia.

Conclusion
From Geevor to Siglo XX and the
lessons of the great tin crash

The collapse of the tin market has affected many mining communities thoughout the world. The situation is stark because of the speed of the changes being imposed by the tin crash. In Bolivia, the effects are particularly harsh because it is already one of the most impoverished countries in the world. Here unemployment can quite literally mean starvation.

In comparing conditions in, for example, Bolivia with what is happening in Cornwall, it is necessary to face the fact that life for workers in England is a great deal easier than in the major tin producing countries. However, the difficulties and hardships imposed on Cornish people stem from the same causes, and the prospects for both groups depend on the same factors. The implication of this is that Bolivian and Cornish workers may be directly in conflict in a game of 'beggar my neighbour'. In the present state of the tin market, saving some mines means closing others. Saving Bolivian production means closure for Cornwall, or some other equally vulnerable producer elsewhere in the world. This is the logic of the market which divides the workers from different mines both within and between countries. The Conservative British government illustrated this when it closed the Geevor tin mine in Cornwall but saved the Wheal Jane and South Crofty mines. The impact of the collapse of tin in Bolivia is more comparable to that of coal mining in Britain. Nevertheless, it is interesting to see how the British government responded to the tin crash. In both cases, the fate of the miners, their families and their communities seems to have had little or no impact on the final decisions taken.

From Geevor...

The stretch of land between St Just and Land's End used to be known as the tin coast. In the nineteenth century, there were 600 mines in

Cornwall; it was the peak period for Cornish tin. Since the depression of the 1870s, the industry has gone through many crises. But towards the end of the 1970s a recovery seemed on the horizon. In 1979, Rio Tinto Zinc bought the shut-down Wheal Jane mine from Consolidated Goldfields and reopened it the following year. Subsequently, it reopened Wheal Maid for development purposes and began refurbishing the South Crofty mine where it bought control in 1985. RTZ invested some £25 million in Cornish tin mining, while Geevor, the only remaining independent mine (in which RTZ had an 18.4 per cent share until February 1986) spent over £1 million per year on modernisation.

Production was soon increasing. It rose from 3,300 tonnes in concentrates in 1976 to over 5,000 in 1985, the highest total since 1918. As Britain was represented on the ITC as a consuming rather than producing nation (because it is not self-sufficient in tin) it did not have to abide by ITC export quotas. Cornwall was therefore able to increase production, taking advantage of the high tin prices the ITC helped maintain. The price collapse was a major blow to all those who had placed hopes on a resurgence of Cornish tin mining.

Geevor's production costs are about £8,500 per tonne, and those of the RTZ mines are between £7,500 and £8,000. A number of problems make the mines high cost; for instance, they are very wet. At the Wheal Jane mine, for every tonne of tin extracted, 4,000 tonnes of water must be pumped out. At the time of the collapse in tin prices, there were plans to reduce costs in all the mines by various capital investment projects. These plans were all brought to a halt when the tin price collapsed and all the Cornish mines plunged into loss. Wheal Maid, which had been opened for exploration purposes only, was immediately closed.

Unlike Bolivia's tin miners, the Cornish miners are not known for their militancy; they were not unionised until the 1950s and mostly belong to the Transport and General Workers' Union rather than the more militant National Union of Mineworkers. The miners work under a contract system and are paid for what they dig. Conditions are very harsh, with temperatures up to 100 degrees Fahrenheit, acid rain, radon gas (which can cause lung cancer) and back-breaking work. But when their jobs were threatened, the miners set about organising a campaign to save the Cornish tin industry.

Miners and management looked to the government for aid when the price of tin collapsed. RTZ, a giant international company with only 1.5 per cent of its huge assets in tin could, as some argued, have afforded to subsidise its mines. It was persuaded to back the modernisation plan put forward by the mines' managing director following his immediate implementation of cost reductions, including an agreement by the workforce to wage freezes for 1985 and 1986. The modernisation programme aimed at cutting costs at the RTZ mines to between £5,100 and £5,300 per tonne, assuming that the world tin price would recover to £6,000 per tonne in ten years. RTZ would not back the plan alone, however; it felt the risks were too high and looked for government assistance.

Geevor sought an interest-free loan of £20 million over five years from the government, also with the aim of reducing tin production costs so that the company could trade profitably at a world tin price of £6,500. The government rejected Geevor's request, but granted a £15 million interest-free loan plus £10 million in loan guarantees to keep the two RTZ mines at Wheal Jane and South Crofty open. Even so, the RTZ mines have only won a breathing space; if there are no profits when the investment programme is complete they will be closed down. The managing director of the mines is fully aware of the risks: 'We are taking a chance. You tell me what the tin price is going to be and I'll tell you if we'll succeed.'

A number of arguments have been put forward in favour of saving the Cornish tin industry and some against. Ultimately the argument which most persuaded the government seems to have been the political cost to the Conservative Party in Cornwall if they had let the Cornish tin industry die. Nevertheless, the argument saved only two Cornish mines. Geevor is already a casualty of the 'Great Tin Crash'.

The tin crisis in Cornwall:
two views

View one: Social need

An interview with an unemployed miner from Geevor

The decision by the Department of Trade and Industry to intervene in the tin crisis in Cornwall has saved the mines owned by Carnon Consolidated (subsidiary of RTZ) — Wheal Jane and South Crofty — from closure at least in the near future. Almost 400 jobs at the independently operated mine, Geevor, will not be saved, however. This wil bring male unemployment in the region of St Just up to 47 per cent. LAB asked one of the unemployed miners at Geevor what his reactions to the tin crisis were.

Q: How do you feel about the government's decision to rescue Wheal Jane and South Crofty, but not Geevor?

Obviously, the Cornish miners are disappointed that the

▶

government has taken so long to do anything at all and has done nothing for Geevor. The government could and should have done a lot more. This is really only a token gesture, made, I think, because they are frightened of unemployment.

At Geevor, the miners' unions have had a good relationship with the management. We have bent over backwards to keep the mine open, even doing overtime without pay. We have behaved in the way this government says unions should, yet we have been cast aside.

The government should have a social conscience. It is not just a question of making money for two or three years. What are the people who have to continue living in this area going to do? Without loans from the government Geevor cannot expand as South Crofty and Wheal Jane will now be able to. We feel very let down.

Q: I believe that you visited the London Metal Exchange last year. What impressions did you receive?

I had not thought about how tin prices were fixed at all before the visit. My first impression was that it is hard to understand how so much money can change hands in such a small space of time. Trading in tin is only limited to a few minutes. It seemed so disorderly.

Then I noticed the people who worked there. They are very young whizz-kid types, professional gamblers really, who live by taking risks. They don't seem to have any understanding of what mining is about for the miners, or the conditions we work in.

I felt quite negative about the visit because the LME looks like a hit-and-miss system, not based on real requirements but on what can be sold in the next three months.

Q: Can you see a future for tin in Britain?

Yes, I can. Tin is a strategic metal with a growing usefulness in the electronics industry. We need tin in this country and we should mine our own instead of importing it.

View two: Economic logic

The tin miners of South Crofty and Wheal Jane in Cornwall have the good luck to live in a part of the country where the Conservative Party is strongly challenged by the Alliance. To shore up the Tory vote, the Thatcher government is giving the miners' multinational employer, Rio Tinto Zinc (RTZ), aid equal to about £40,000 for each of the 640 jobs it purports to save. The deal may make short-term electoral sense in a county where male unemployment is

▶

95

running at 25 per cent in some villages. Economically, it is nonsense...

Since RTZ naturally likes to be subsidised, it has tried to present more than a political case for keeping its tin miners digging. With the government's money, it says, it can reduce the cost of producing tin in Cornwall to about £5,000 a tonne, from the £7,000 it is put at today by independent assessors...

That argument conveniently overlooks an obvious doubt: if this investment really could reduce unit costs by 25-30 per cent, profit-seeking RTZ would have undertaken it long ago. And even if Cornish costs were to be slashed, they would still not be competitive. Malaysia, the largest producer, has many tin operations that can be profitably prolific at £4,500 a tonne (at today's exchange rates). Production in Brazil is increasing rapidly... Add to this the hundreds of small Malaysian and Thai operations that will come back into business if the tin price recovers to £5,000 — it does not take long to restart a tin dredge — and the loans to RTZ look a foolish way to add to what, at £5,000 a tonne, would be an unsustainable tin surplus.

The chances are high that the Cornish tin industry will be back queueing for more aid at the government trough before the decade is out, as bankers sell the 100,000 tonnes of tin they now unwillingly hold and as other countries strive to keep marginal mines in business. Indonesia already subsidises its tin producers. Malaysia has promised to pay its producers the difference between £4,500 and the price they can realise on world markets. The sooner the uneconomic Cornish tin mines follow uneconomic coal mines into closure, the better for poor developing counties, the British taxpayer and the British economy.

The Economist, 16 August 1986

... to Siglo XX

Some third world governments are perfectly willing to implement changes enforced by the world market without taking account of the human suffering generated as a result; they may hope to gain favourable loans or aid from the international agencies which support such changes. Governments which can rely on military power to support their decisions do not have to listen to the voice of their dispossessed.

The Bolivian miners have few weapons to resist the forces against them. Dynamite cannot defeat the world market. They have produced a plan which is coherent in the longer term but which will not deal with the immediate crisis. The failure of the traditional pattern of Bolivian development based on dependence on the fortunes of one or two commodities has been clearly demonstrated by the history of tin. A serious search for alternatives is an urgent task, but in the meantime Bolivia needs to maintain what productive potential it has in order to ease the transition to new economic activities.

The miners' plan at least addresses the issue of Bolivia's productive base and the importance of state intervention to maintain it. The government only offers neo-liberal economic solutions, widely discredited in Chile and elsewhere where they have been applied. It looks to international financial agencies, foreign and local private capital to rescue the economy, but offers no strategy for the country's long-term future aimed at meeting the basic needs of the people. The difficulties facing Bolivia's tin industry had been known for some time before the crash. The government is now using the crash to implement political solutions with an apparent economic logic; its priority is to destroy the power of the country's tin miners.

With US troops now on Bolivian soil in an effort to stamp out cocaine production, almost the only remaining source of employment and income for thousands of peasants and many ex-miners is at risk. But so far neither the Bolivian government nor the US administration has come up with alternatives for those left destitute.

Thousands of miners have given their lives to produce the mineral which for many years was the country's lifeblood. An estimated 25,000 Comibol employees have contracted silicosis since 1956; several thousand more have died in mining accidents or as a result of government repression; average life expectancy amongst miners is 35 years. The miners have a right to a say in the future of the industry. But they will still have to fight to exercise that right. For decades the miners have led the struggle of Bolivia's urban and rural workers to build a society which represents their interests. Today, the miners as well as the very future of Bolivia are at the crossroads.

Lessons of the great tin crash

1. Safeguarding the stabilisation mechanism

As was argued in chapter 3, the tin agreement did not lead to the crash of the tin market. This came about because the market stabilisation mechanism (ie the buffer stock) was financed in a high-risk way, more suitable to the financing of a new individual mining project. When it came unstuck it brought down the entire market causing huge losses worldwide. The main lesson of the crash, for those concerned with the technical design of commodity agreements, is that the stabilisation mechanism must itself be safeguarded from extreme pressures.

2. Shouldering the blame

This high-risk means of financing was in use because the rich consumer countries refused to shoulder the burden which only they could bear and to provide the finance needed for the tin agreement to work effectively. The system's control mechanism (ie the buffer stock) was made unreliable; the situation was equivalent to placing a central heating thermostat actually on a radiator. In this way, the rich consumer countries created the conditions for the great tin crash.

Adjustments to the oversupply in the tin market were taking place before the crash, major producers were cutting back on production. If these had been allowed to happen gradually through a properly funded ITC, much hardship could have been spared for the mining communities around the world. Through their failure to maintain stable exchange rates and their refusal to help the ITC when currency fluctuations brought about the tin crash, the rich countries bear considerable responsibility for this hardship.

3. Sharing the cost of change

The excess capacity which exists in the tin industry is not peculiar. In other commodities and also in many areas of industrial production, there are massive surpluses of productive resources available. There are shifts occurring in the international pattern of production whose effects are visible in the huge number of people unemployed in the older industrialised countries. These changes involve production being shut down in some countries as others increase output. Changes in technology and in the pattern of demand are accompanying recession. These involve adjustments which mean unemployment and often poverty and misery for many. The sensible management of such changes requires providing protection for its victims. The advanced industrialised countries have social security systems, compulsory redundancy benefits and so on. In the face of growing demand, these social services are under heavy strain and increasingly unable to meet the needs of the people affected — the long-term unemployed, for instance. These problems are immeasurably increased in the case of poor countries such as Bolivia.

The crisis of Bolivia's tin industry can be compared with what has happened to Britain's coal industry. Since 1947, some 500,000 jobs have gone in the coal industry. But until the Thatcher government came to power in 1979, subsidies and the creation of alternatives made this process less painful for the workers. Since the NUM lost its battle with the government in 1985, 30,000 miners have lost their jobs; 60,000 jobs were lost between 1983 and 1986. The scale of the present crisis facing Bolivia is similar.

A solution is needed not only for the recovery from the present depths of the crisis in tin but for the general management of the process of change. The process of change is the source of the increasing wealth of the industrialised nations and of the world as a whole. This is true for socialist as well as capitalist economies. Under capitalism, however, not only are the benefits not shared but the very process of change itself generates losses and hardship to its victims. National governments in the third world do not have the resources to compensate their citizens for changes in the international division of labour. The tin crash has shown the importance of sharing the costs of a crisis of this dimension equitably, with wealthy consumer nations assuming more of the burden.

4. The future of commodity agreements

The collapse of the ITC is being used by those who would like to leave everything to the market to discredit all commodity agreements. The existence of the tin agreement itself is being blamed for the collapse of the market, by maintaining prices which led to oversupply. It is possible to detect a certain annoyance here with the tin producers who did not let the price of their product fall in the way that other commodities did (and incidentally, pay for the end of inflation in the industrialised world). Bolivian tin miners who live on starvation wages and work in appalling conditions would no doubt be incredulous at the suggestion that the price of tin had been kept too high. But in the discussions taking place in November 1986 on the international rubber agreement, the case of tin was used to discredit the idea that floor prices should be set to guarantee export incomes for producers. The practical implications of this argument are to abolish the fixed floor price for intervention and to make the floor price itself move up and down with the state of the market, thus removing price guarantees for the producer.

Those who argue against commodity agreements are ignoring the instabilities generated by the structure and operation of large-scale mineral production. The difficulty is to convince governments operating under domestic political pressures to make sensible agreements. It is easier for governments to impose domestic changes by blaming uncontrollable international forces, ie the market. In this way, the British government can avoid responsibility for the closure of Geevor.

But ultimately, stabilisation mechanisms like the ITA make sense in today's commodity markets. Both producers and consumers need stable markets and stable trading relations. A new international tin agreement should be speedily arranged. New financing for tin and the re-creation of the stockpile to take current excesses off the market are needed. Such action would alleviate some of the immediate problems facing the tin industry around the world, while allowing time for the necessary adjustments to the problems of oversupply.

But this is only part of the problem. The other is how to use commodity agreements to increase the income of third world producers. Rich countries could afford to pay more for their tin; those who produce the tin have standards of living far below workers in the industrialised countries and work in conditions which they would never tolerate. There are sound economic arguments for commodity agreements, and very strong moral ones for using them to secure a fairer deal for the poor producers.

Western governments who oppose the use of high commodity prices to redistribute income to the third world see such a mechanism as at best an inefficient method of giving aid. Some argue that higher commodity prices benefit mine owners and not the poor. Aid, however, is not what is at issue, but a genuine transfer of economic power and wealth. Aid is a tool used by western governments to both assist their own economies, to gain influence in third world countries and even to actually control events in those countries. UNCTAD sought to break this by providing new means to transfer resources.

Inside individual nations there is a distribution of natural resources, just as on the world stage. Because prices are set for the whole market, whole markets receive the same price — the cheapest producer as well as the most expensive (marginal) producer. The first is able to make large profits, while the latter gets very little. What happens in many countries is that the state then taxes away these extra profits, and this is what must happen in third world countries for the poor to benefit.

No such mechanism operates on the world level. There is no means of taking away the extra profit from the low-cost producers in Brazil and sending them to help the Bolivian miners. More fundamentally, of course, there is no means of taxing the high-productivity industrialised countries to help the third world.

Given the present world economic order the most that commodity agreements can do is to ensure that adjustment costs are shared between countries. In other words, they can soften the harsher blows of the market. They cannot eliminate its impact altogether. Nor can commodity agreements by themselves guarantee that benefits from stable or higher prices go to those most in need within a poor producer country. A transfer of wealth and power must take place within many third world nations as well as between them and the industrialised world if the causes of poverty are to be seriously tackled. Ultimately, although they have an important role to play, commodity agreements cannot substitute for a planned world economy geared to ensuring a minimum standard of living for all, in which the costs as well as the benefits of change are shared.

Jenny Matthews

Selected bibliography

Annual Review of the World Tin Industry, London, Shearson Lehman Brothers, 1984 and 1985

Ayub, Mahmood Ali and Hideo Hasimoto, *The Economics of Tin Mining in Bolivia*, Washington DC, Word Bank, 1985

Barrios de Chungara, Domitila, *Let Me Speak! Testimony of Domitila, a Woman of the Bolivian Mines*, New York, Monthly Review Press, 1978

Bolivia Bulletin, La Paz, CEDOIN

CEDOIN, *Los Mineros de Ayer y de Hoy*, La Paz, October 1986

Dalton, Alan, 'Mine closures in Cornwall: out of our control', *International Labour Report*, Manchester

Dunkerley, James, *Rebellion in the Veins: Political Struggle in Bolivia 1952-82*, London, Verso Editions, 1984

Fox, David J, *Mines and Mining in the Americas*, Manchester, Manchester University Press, 1985

Galeano, Eduardo, *Open Veins of Latin America: Five Centuries of the Pillage of a Continent*, New York, Monthly Review Press, 1973

House of Commons Select Committee on Trade and Industry Report, *The Tin Crisis*, London, HMSO, 1986

Informe 'R', CEDOIN, La Paz

International Tin Council, *Monthly Statistical Summary*

Labour Research, London

Latin America Bureau, *Bolivia: Coup d'Etat*, London, 1980

Latin American Mining Letter, London

Lora, Guillermo, *A History of the Bolivian Labour Movement 1948-1971*, Cambridge, Cambridge University Press, 1977

Martin, Gail, 'Carrying the can: Bolivian labour and the international tin crisis', *Journal of Area Studies*, No 13, Spring 1986, Portsmouth Polytechnic School of Languages and Area Studies

Mayo, E.G. and Casteel, K.D., *The changing face of Latin America's tin Industry and its effect on the world tin market*, Metals and Minerals Publications Ltd, London, 1986

Metals Analysis and Outlook, London, 1986

National Union of Mineworkers, *Trade Union and Human Rights in Chile and Bolivia*, Report of the NUM Delegation, London, 1977

National Union of Mineworkers, *Report of an NUM Delegation, London, July 1979*

St Ives Constituency Labour Party, *The tin crisis and Geevor: a brief guide*

Tin International, London, Metals and Minerals Publications Ltd

Other LAB Publications

Paraguay: Power Game
September 1980. 76pp. £1.50

**Under the Eagle: US Intervention in Central America
and the Caribbean**
by Jenny Pearce
Updated edition April 1982. 295pp. £5.95

**The European Challenge: Europe's New
Role in Latin America**
June 1982. 244pp. £3.95

Guyana: Fraudulent Revolution
March 1984. 106pp. £3.50

Grenada: Whose Freedom?
by Fitzroy Ambursley and James Dunkerley
April 1984. 128pp. £3.50

Peru: Paths to Poverty
by Michael Reid
February 1985. 136pp. £3.50

Haiti: Family Business
by Rod Prince
September 1985. 86pp. £3.50

Honduras: State for Sale
by Richard Lapper and James Painter
November 1985. 132pp. £3.50

**Promised Land: Peasant Rebellion in Chalatenango,
El Salvador**
by Jenny Pearce
March 1986. 320pp. £6.95

Prices do not include postage